C-3221   CAREER EXAMINATION SERIES

This is your
PASSBOOK for...

Account Clerk-Typist

Test Preparation Study Guide
Questions & Answers

NATIONAL LEARNING CORPORATION®

COPYRIGHT NOTICE

This book is SOLELY intended for, is sold ONLY to, and its use is RESTRICTED to individual, bona fide applicants or candidates who qualify by virtue of having seriously filed applications for appropriate license, certificate, professional and/or promotional advancement, higher school matriculation, scholarship, or other legitimate requirements of education and/or governmental authorities.

This book is NOT intended for use, class instruction, tutoring, training, duplication, copying, reprinting, excerption, or adaptation, etc., by:

1) Other publishers
2) Proprietors and/or Instructors of "Coaching" and/or Preparatory Courses
3) Personnel and/or Training Divisions of commercial, industrial, and governmental organizations
4) Schools, colleges, or universities and/or their departments and staffs, including teachers and other personnel
5) Testing Agencies or Bureaus
6) Study groups which seek by the purchase of a single volume to copy and/or duplicate and/or adapt this material for use by the group as a whole without having purchased individual volumes for each of the members of the group
7) Et al.

Such persons would be in violation of appropriate Federal and State statutes.

PROVISION OF LICENSING AGREEMENTS – Recognized educational, commercial, industrial, and governmental institutions and organizations, and others legitimately engaged in educational pursuits, including training, testing, and measurement activities, may address request for a licensing agreement to the copyright owners, who will determine whether, and under what conditions, including fees and charges, the materials in this book may be used them. In other words, a licensing facility exists for the legitimate use of the material in this book on other than an individual basis. However, it is asseverated and affirmed here that the material in this book CANNOT be used without the receipt of the express permission of such a licensing agreement from the Publishers. Inquiries re licensing should be addressed to the company, attention rights and permissions department.

All rights reserved, including the right of reproduction in whole or in part, in any form or by any means, electronic or mechanical, including photocopying, recording, or by any information storage and retrieval system, without permission in writing from the Publisher.

Copyright © 2024 by
National Learning Corporation

212 Michael Drive, Syosset, NY 11791
(516) 921-8888 • www.passbooks.com
E-mail: info@passbooks.com

PUBLISHED IN THE UNITED STATES OF AMERICA

PASSBOOK® SERIES

THE *PASSBOOK® SERIES* has been created to prepare applicants and candidates for the ultimate academic battlefield – the examination room.

At some time in our lives, each and every one of us may be required to take an examination – for validation, matriculation, admission, qualification, registration, certification, or licensure.

Based on the assumption that every applicant or candidate has met the basic formal educational standards, has taken the required number of courses, and read the necessary texts, the *PASSBOOK® SERIES* furnishes the one special preparation which may assure passing with confidence, instead of failing with insecurity. Examination questions – together with answers – are furnished as the basic vehicle for study so that the mysteries of the examination and its compounding difficulties may be eliminated or diminished by a sure method.

This book is meant to help you pass your examination provided that you qualify and are serious in your objective.

The entire field is reviewed through the huge store of content information which is succinctly presented through a provocative and challenging approach – the question-and-answer method.

A climate of success is established by furnishing the correct answers at the end of each test.

You soon learn to recognize types of questions, forms of questions, and patterns of questioning. You may even begin to anticipate expected outcomes.

You perceive that many questions are repeated or adapted so that you can gain acute insights, which may enable you to score many sure points.

You learn how to confront new questions, or types of questions, and to attack them confidently and work out the correct answers.

You note objectives and emphases, and recognize pitfalls and dangers, so that you may make positive educational adjustments.

Moreover, you are kept fully informed in relation to new concepts, methods, practices, and directions in the field.

You discover that you are actually taking the examination all the time: you are preparing for the examination by "taking" an examination, not by reading extraneous and/or supererogatory textbooks.

In short, this PASSBOOK®, used directedly, should be an important factor in helping you to pass your test.

ACCOUNT CLERK/TYPIST

DUTIES:
This is routine clerical work involving the performance of standardized account-keeping tasks in maintaining and checking financial accounts and records. The incumbent enters and retrieves account information manually or by using computer database and/or spreadsheet software. Work is performed under the direct supervision of a higher level employee in accordance with well defined policies and procedures. Additionally, the incumbent will be responsible for entering and retrieving information from a computer database and using a computer or word processor to produce printed material such as forms, letters and memoranda. The incumbent works under supervision on routine assignments that are done in accordance with defined procedures; detailed instructions are provided for new or unusual assignments.

The positions of Account Clerk and Account Clerk/Typist differ in that an Account Clerk/Typist spends significantly more time operating and alphanumeric keyboard such as a typewriter, word processor or personal computer to perform typing work which requires a qualified typist. This class differs from Senior Account Clerk by virtue of the limited complexity of the work. The work is reviewed by observation, crosschecks, or by the immediate supervisor and by other steps in the account-keeping process. Does related work as required.

SCOPE OF THE EXAMINATION
The written test is designed to test a candidate's knowledge, skills and/or abilities in such areas as:
1. **Clerical Operations with Letters and Numbers** - These questions test your skills and abilities in clerical operations involving alphabetizing, comparing, checking and counting. The questions require you to follow the specific directions given for each question which may involve alphabetizing, comparing, checking and counting given groups of letters and/or numbers.
2. **Arithmetic Computation Without Calculators** -These questions test your ability to do addition, subtraction, multiplication, and division. Questions may also involve fractions, decimals, averages, and percents.
3. **Arithmetic Reasoning** - These questions test your ability to solve an arithmetic problem presented in sentence or short paragraph form. You must read the problem, understand the situation presented, decide what must be done to solve it, and apply the appropriate arithmetic operation(s) in the appropriate order in order to determine the correct solution. Knowledge of addition, subtraction, multiplication and division is necessary. Questions may also involve the use of percents, decimals and fractions.

HOW TO TAKE A TEST

I. YOU MUST PASS AN EXAMINATION

A. *WHAT EVERY CANDIDATE SHOULD KNOW*

Examination applicants often ask us for help in preparing for the written test. What can I study in advance? What kinds of questions will be asked? How will the test be given? How will the papers be graded?

As an applicant for a civil service examination, you may be wondering about some of these things. Our purpose here is to suggest effective methods of advance study and to describe civil service examinations.

Your chances for success on this examination can be increased if you know how to prepare. Those "pre-examination jitters" can be reduced if you know what to expect. You can even experience an adventure in good citizenship if you know why civil service exams are given.

B. *WHY ARE CIVIL SERVICE EXAMINATIONS GIVEN?*

Civil service examinations are important to you in two ways. As a citizen, you want public jobs filled by employees who know how to do their work. As a job seeker, you want a fair chance to compete for that job on an equal footing with other candidates. The best-known means of accomplishing this two-fold goal is the competitive examination.

Exams are widely publicized throughout the nation. They may be administered for jobs in federal, state, city, municipal, town or village governments or agencies.

Any citizen may apply, with some limitations, such as the age or residence of applicants. Your experience and education may be reviewed to see whether you meet the requirements for the particular examination. When these requirements exist, they are reasonable and applied consistently to all applicants. Thus, a competitive examination may cause you some uneasiness now, but it is your privilege and safeguard.

C. *HOW ARE CIVIL SERVICE EXAMS DEVELOPED?*

Examinations are carefully written by trained technicians who are specialists in the field known as "psychological measurement," in consultation with recognized authorities in the field of work that the test will cover. These experts recommend the subject matter areas or skills to be tested; only those knowledges or skills important to your success on the job are included. The most reliable books and source materials available are used as references. Together, the experts and technicians judge the difficulty level of the questions.

Test technicians know how to phrase questions so that the problem is clearly stated. Their ethics do not permit "trick" or "catch" questions. Questions may have been tried out on sample groups, or subjected to statistical analysis, to determine their usefulness.

Written tests are often used in combination with performance tests, ratings of training and experience, and oral interviews. All of these measures combine to form the best-known means of finding the right person for the right job.

II. HOW TO PASS THE WRITTEN TEST

A. NATURE OF THE EXAMINATION

To prepare intelligently for civil service examinations, you should know how they differ from school examinations you have taken. In school you were assigned certain definite pages to read or subjects to cover. The examination questions were quite detailed and usually emphasized memory. Civil service exams, on the other hand, try to discover your present ability to perform the duties of a position, plus your potentiality to learn these duties. In other words, a civil service exam attempts to predict how successful you will be. Questions cover such a broad area that they cannot be as minute and detailed as school exam questions.

In the public service similar kinds of work, or positions, are grouped together in one "class." This process is known as *position-classification*. All the positions in a class are paid according to the salary range for that class. One class title covers all of these positions, and they are all tested by the same examination.

B. FOUR BASIC STEPS

1) Study the announcement

How, then, can you know what subjects to study? Our best answer is: "Learn as much as possible about the class of positions for which you've applied." The exam will test the knowledge, skills and abilities needed to do the work.

Your most valuable source of information about the position you want is the official exam announcement. This announcement lists the training and experience qualifications. Check these standards and apply only if you come reasonably close to meeting them.

The brief description of the position in the examination announcement offers some clues to the subjects which will be tested. Think about the job itself. Review the duties in your mind. Can you perform them, or are there some in which you are rusty? Fill in the blank spots in your preparation.

Many jurisdictions preview the written test in the exam announcement by including a section called "Knowledge and Abilities Required," "Scope of the Examination," or some similar heading. Here you will find out specifically what fields will be tested.

2) Review your own background

Once you learn in general what the position is all about, and what you need to know to do the work, ask yourself which subjects you already know fairly well and which need improvement. You may wonder whether to concentrate on improving your strong areas or on building some background in your fields of weakness. When the announcement has specified "some knowledge" or "considerable knowledge," or has used adjectives like "beginning principles of..." or "advanced ... methods," you can get a clue as to the number and difficulty of questions to be asked in any given field. More questions, and hence broader coverage, would be included for those subjects which are more important in the work. Now weigh your strengths and weaknesses against the job requirements and prepare accordingly.

3) Determine the level of the position

Another way to tell how intensively you should prepare is to understand the level of the job for which you are applying. Is it the entering level? In other words, is this the position in which beginners in a field of work are hired? Or is it an intermediate or advanced level? Sometimes this is indicated by such words as "Junior" or "Senior" in the class title. Other jurisdictions use Roman numerals to designate the level – Clerk I, Clerk II, for example. The word "Supervisor" sometimes appears in the title. If the level is not indicated by the title, check the description of duties. Will you be working under very close supervision, or will you have responsibility for independent decisions in this work?

4) Choose appropriate study materials

Now that you know the subjects to be examined and the relative amount of each subject to be covered, you can choose suitable study materials. For beginning level jobs, or even advanced ones, if you have a pronounced weakness in some aspect of your training, read a modern, standard textbook in that field. Be sure it is up to date and has general coverage. Such books are normally available at your library, and the librarian will be glad to help you locate one. For entry-level positions, questions of appropriate difficulty are chosen – neither highly advanced questions, nor those too simple. Such questions require careful thought but not advanced training.

If the position for which you are applying is technical or advanced, you will read more advanced, specialized material. If you are already familiar with the basic principles of your field, elementary textbooks would waste your time. Concentrate on advanced textbooks and technical periodicals. Think through the concepts and review difficult problems in your field.

These are all general sources. You can get more ideas on your own initiative, following these leads. For example, training manuals and publications of the government agency which employs workers in your field can be useful, particularly for technical and professional positions. A letter or visit to the government department involved may result in more specific study suggestions, and certainly will provide you with a more definite idea of the exact nature of the position you are seeking.

III. KINDS OF TESTS

Tests are used for purposes other than measuring knowledge and ability to perform specified duties. For some positions, it is equally important to test ability to make adjustments to new situations or to profit from training. In others, basic mental abilities not dependent on information are essential. Questions which test these things may not appear as pertinent to the duties of the position as those which test for knowledge and information. Yet they are often highly important parts of a fair examination. For very general questions, it is almost impossible to help you direct your study efforts. What we can do is to point out some of the more common of these general abilities needed in public service positions and describe some typical questions.

1) General information

Broad, general information has been found useful for predicting job success in some kinds of work. This is tested in a variety of ways, from vocabulary lists to questions about current events. Basic background in some field of work, such as sociology or economics, may be sampled in a group of questions. Often these are principles which have become familiar to most persons through exposure rather than through formal training. It is difficult to advise you how to study for these questions; being alert to the world around you is our best suggestion.

2) Verbal ability

An example of an ability needed in many positions is verbal or language ability. Verbal ability is, in brief, the ability to use and understand words. Vocabulary and grammar tests are typical measures of this ability. Reading comprehension or paragraph interpretation questions are common in many kinds of civil service tests. You are given a paragraph of written material and asked to find its central meaning.

3) Numerical ability

Number skills can be tested by the familiar arithmetic problem, by checking paired lists of numbers to see which are alike and which are different, or by interpreting charts and graphs. In the latter test, a graph may be printed in the test booklet which you are asked to use as the basis for answering questions.

4) Observation

A popular test for law-enforcement positions is the observation test. A picture is shown to you for several minutes, then taken away. Questions about the picture test your ability to observe both details and larger elements.

5) Following directions

In many positions in the public service, the employee must be able to carry out written instructions dependably and accurately. You may be given a chart with several columns, each column listing a variety of information. The questions require you to carry out directions involving the information given in the chart.

6) Skills and aptitudes

Performance tests effectively measure some manual skills and aptitudes. When the skill is one in which you are trained, such as typing or shorthand, you can practice. These tests are often very much like those given in business school or high school courses. For many of the other skills and aptitudes, however, no short-time preparation can be made. Skills and abilities natural to you or that you have developed throughout your lifetime are being tested.

Many of the general questions just described provide all the data needed to answer the questions and ask you to use your reasoning ability to find the answers. Your best preparation for these tests, as well as for tests of facts and ideas, is to be at your physical and mental best. You, no doubt, have your own methods of getting into an exam-taking mood and keeping "in shape." The next section lists some ideas on this subject.

IV. KINDS OF QUESTIONS

Only rarely is the "essay" question, which you answer in narrative form, used in civil service tests. Civil service tests are usually of the short-answer type. Full instructions for answering these questions will be given to you at the examination. But in case this is your first experience with short-answer questions and separate answer sheets, here is what you need to know:

1) Multiple-choice Questions

Most popular of the short-answer questions is the "multiple choice" or "best answer" question. It can be used, for example, to test for factual knowledge, ability to solve problems or judgment in meeting situations found at work.

A multiple-choice question is normally one of three types—
- It can begin with an incomplete statement followed by several possible endings. You are to find the one ending which *best* completes the statement, although some of the others may not be entirely wrong.
- It can also be a complete statement in the form of a question which is answered by choosing one of the statements listed.

- It can be in the form of a problem – again you select the best answer.

Here is an example of a multiple-choice question with a discussion which should give you some clues as to the method for choosing the right answer:

When an employee has a complaint about his assignment, the action which will *best* help him overcome his difficulty is to
    A. discuss his difficulty with his coworkers
    B. take the problem to the head of the organization
    C. take the problem to the person who gave him the assignment
    D. say nothing to anyone about his complaint

In answering this question, you should study each of the choices to find which is best. Consider choice "A" – Certainly an employee may discuss his complaint with fellow employees, but no change or improvement can result, and the complaint remains unresolved. Choice "B" is a poor choice since the head of the organization probably does not know what assignment you have been given, and taking your problem to him is known as "going over the head" of the supervisor. The supervisor, or person who made the assignment, is the person who can clarify it or correct any injustice. Choice "C" is, therefore, correct. To say nothing, as in choice "D," is unwise. Supervisors have and interest in knowing the problems employees are facing, and the employee is seeking a solution to his problem.

2) True/False Questions

The "true/false" or "right/wrong" form of question is sometimes used. Here a complete statement is given. Your job is to decide whether the statement is right or wrong.

SAMPLE: A roaming cell-phone call to a nearby city costs less than a non-roaming call to a distant city.

This statement is wrong, or false, since roaming calls are more expensive.
This is not a complete list of all possible question forms, although most of the others are variations of these common types. You will always get complete directions for answering questions. Be sure you understand *how* to mark your answers – ask questions until you do.

V. RECORDING YOUR ANSWERS

Computer terminals are used more and more today for many different kinds of exams.
For an examination with very few applicants, you may be told to record your answers in the test booklet itself. Separate answer sheets are much more common. If this separate answer sheet is to be scored by machine – and this is often the case – it is highly important that you mark your answers correctly in order to get credit.
An electronic scoring machine is often used in civil service offices because of the speed with which papers can be scored. Machine-scored answer sheets must be marked with a pencil, which will be given to you. This pencil has a high graphite content which responds to the electronic scoring machine. As a matter of fact, stray dots may register as answers, so do not let your pencil rest on the answer sheet while you are pondering the correct answer. Also, if your pencil lead breaks or is otherwise defective, ask for another.

Since the answer sheet will be dropped in a slot in the scoring machine, be careful not to bend the corners or get the paper crumpled.

The answer sheet normally has five vertical columns of numbers, with 30 numbers to a column. These numbers correspond to the question numbers in your test booklet. After each number, going across the page are four or five pairs of dotted lines. These short dotted lines have small letters or numbers above them. The first two pairs may also have a "T" or "F" above the letters. This indicates that the first two pairs only are to be used if the questions are of the true-false type. If the questions are multiple choice, disregard the "T" and "F" and pay attention only to the small letters or numbers.

Answer your questions in the manner of the sample that follows:

32. The largest city in the United States is
    A. Washington, D.C.
    B. New York City
    C. Chicago
    D. Detroit
    E. San Francisco

1) Choose the answer you think is best. (New York City is the largest, so "B" is correct.)
2) Find the row of dotted lines numbered the same as the question you are answering. (Find row number 32)
3) Find the pair of dotted lines corresponding to the answer. (Find the pair of lines under the mark "B.")
4) Make a solid black mark between the dotted lines.

VI. BEFORE THE TEST

Common sense will help you find procedures to follow to get ready for an examination. Too many of us, however, overlook these sensible measures. Indeed, nervousness and fatigue have been found to be the most serious reasons why applicants fail to do their best on civil service tests. Here is a list of reminders:

- Begin your preparation early – Don't wait until the last minute to go scurrying around for books and materials or to find out what the position is all about.
- Prepare continuously – An hour a night for a week is better than an all-night cram session. This has been definitely established. What is more, a night a week for a month will return better dividends than crowding your study into a shorter period of time.
- Locate the place of the exam – You have been sent a notice telling you when and where to report for the examination. If the location is in a different town or otherwise unfamiliar to you, it would be well to inquire the best route and learn something about the building.
- Relax the night before the test – Allow your mind to rest. Do not study at all that night. Plan some mild recreation or diversion; then go to bed early and get a good night's sleep.
- Get up early enough to make a leisurely trip to the place for the test – This way unforeseen events, traffic snarls, unfamiliar buildings, etc. will not upset you.
- Dress comfortably – A written test is not a fashion show. You will be known by number and not by name, so wear something comfortable.

- Leave excess paraphernalia at home – Shopping bags and odd bundles will get in your way. You need bring only the items mentioned in the official notice you received; usually everything you need is provided. Do not bring reference books to the exam. They will only confuse those last minutes and be taken away from you when in the test room.
- Arrive somewhat ahead of time – If because of transportation schedules you must get there very early, bring a newspaper or magazine to take your mind off yourself while waiting.
- Locate the examination room – When you have found the proper room, you will be directed to the seat or part of the room where you will sit. Sometimes you are given a sheet of instructions to read while you are waiting. Do not fill out any forms until you are told to do so; just read them and be prepared.
- Relax and prepare to listen to the instructions
- If you have any physical problem that may keep you from doing your best, be sure to tell the test administrator. If you are sick or in poor health, you really cannot do your best on the exam. You can come back and take the test some other time.

VII. AT THE TEST

The day of the test is here and you have the test booklet in your hand. The temptation to get going is very strong. Caution! There is more to success than knowing the right answers. You must know how to identify your papers and understand variations in the type of short-answer question used in this particular examination. Follow these suggestions for maximum results from your efforts:

1) Cooperate with the monitor

The test administrator has a duty to create a situation in which you can be as much at ease as possible. He will give instructions, tell you when to begin, check to see that you are marking your answer sheet correctly, and so on. He is not there to guard you, although he will see that your competitors do not take unfair advantage. He wants to help you do your best.

2) Listen to all instructions

Don't jump the gun! Wait until you understand all directions. In most civil service tests you get more time than you need to answer the questions. So don't be in a hurry. Read each word of instructions until you clearly understand the meaning. Study the examples, listen to all announcements and follow directions. Ask questions if you do not understand what to do.

3) Identify your papers

Civil service exams are usually identified by number only. You will be assigned a number; you must not put your name on your test papers. Be sure to copy your number correctly. Since more than one exam may be given, copy your exact examination title.

4) Plan your time

Unless you are told that a test is a "speed" or "rate of work" test, speed itself is usually not important. Time enough to answer all the questions will be provided, but this does not mean that you have all day. An overall time limit has been set. Divide the total time (in minutes) by the number of questions to determine the approximate time you have for each question.

5) Do not linger over difficult questions

If you come across a difficult question, mark it with a paper clip (useful to have along) and come back to it when you have been through the booklet. One caution if you do this – be sure to skip a number on your answer sheet as well. Check often to be sure that you have not lost your place and that you are marking in the row numbered the same as the question you are answering.

6) Read the questions

Be sure you know what the question asks! Many capable people are unsuccessful because they failed to *read* the questions correctly.

7) Answer all questions

Unless you have been instructed that a penalty will be deducted for incorrect answers, it is better to guess than to omit a question.

8) Speed tests

It is often better NOT to guess on speed tests. It has been found that on timed tests people are tempted to spend the last few seconds before time is called in marking answers at random – without even reading them – in the hope of picking up a few extra points. To discourage this practice, the instructions may warn you that your score will be "corrected" for guessing. That is, a penalty will be applied. The incorrect answers will be deducted from the correct ones, or some other penalty formula will be used.

9) Review your answers

If you finish before time is called, go back to the questions you guessed or omitted to give them further thought. Review other answers if you have time.

10) Return your test materials

If you are ready to leave before others have finished or time is called, take ALL your materials to the monitor and leave quietly. Never take any test material with you. The monitor can discover whose papers are not complete, and taking a test booklet may be grounds for disqualification.

VIII. EXAMINATION TECHNIQUES

1) Read the general instructions carefully. These are usually printed on the first page of the exam booklet. As a rule, these instructions refer to the timing of the examination; the fact that you should not start work until the signal and must stop work at a signal, etc. If there are any *special* instructions, such as a choice of questions to be answered, make sure that you note this instruction carefully.

2) When you are ready to start work on the examination, that is as soon as the signal has been given, read the instructions to each question booklet, underline any key words or phrases, such as *least, best, outline, describe* and the like. In this way you will tend to answer as requested rather than discover on reviewing your paper that you *listed without describing*, that you selected the *worst* choice rather than the *best* choice, etc.

3) If the examination is of the objective or multiple-choice type – that is, each question will also give a series of possible answers: A, B, C or D, and you are called upon to select the best answer and write the letter next to that answer on your answer paper – it is advisable to start answering each question in turn. There may be anywhere from 50 to 100 such questions in the three or four hours allotted and you can see how much time would be taken if you read through all the questions before beginning to answer any. Furthermore, if you come across a question or group of questions which you know would be difficult to answer, it would undoubtedly affect your handling of all the other questions.

4) If the examination is of the essay type and contains but a few questions, it is a moot point as to whether you should read all the questions before starting to answer any one. Of course, if you are given a choice – say five out of seven and the like – then it is essential to read all the questions so you can eliminate the two that are most difficult. If, however, you are asked to answer all the questions, there may be danger in trying to answer the easiest one first because you may find that you will spend too much time on it. The best technique is to answer the first question, then proceed to the second, etc.

5) Time your answers. Before the exam begins, write down the time it started, then add the time allowed for the examination and write down the time it must be completed, then divide the time available somewhat as follows:
    - If 3-1/2 hours are allowed, that would be 210 minutes. If you have 80 objective-type questions, that would be an average of 2-1/2 minutes per question. Allow yourself no more than 2 minutes per question, or a total of 160 minutes, which will permit about 50 minutes to review.
    - If for the time allotment of 210 minutes there are 7 essay questions to answer, that would average about 30 minutes a question. Give yourself only 25 minutes per question so that you have about 35 minutes to review.

6) The most important instruction is to *read each question* and make sure you know what is wanted. The second most important instruction is to *time yourself properly* so that you answer every question. The third most important instruction is to *answer every question*. Guess if you have to but include something for each question. Remember that you will receive no credit for a blank and will probably receive some credit if you write something in answer to an essay question. If you guess a letter – say "B" for a multiple-choice question – you may have guessed right. If you leave a blank as an answer to a multiple-choice question, the examiners may respect your feelings but it will not add a point to your score. Some exams may penalize you for wrong answers, so in such cases *only*, you may not want to guess unless you have some basis for your answer.

7) Suggestions
    a. Objective-type questions
        1. Examine the question booklet for proper sequence of pages and questions
        2. Read all instructions carefully
        3. Skip any question which seems too difficult; return to it after all other questions have been answered
        4. Apportion your time properly; do not spend too much time on any single question or group of questions

5. Note and underline key words – *all, most, fewest, least, best, worst, same, opposite*, etc.
6. Pay particular attention to negatives
7. Note unusual option, e.g., unduly long, short, complex, different or similar in content to the body of the question
8. Observe the use of "hedging" words – *probably, may, most likely*, etc.
9. Make sure that your answer is put next to the same number as the question
10. Do not second-guess unless you have good reason to believe the second answer is definitely more correct
11. Cross out original answer if you decide another answer is more accurate; do not erase until you are ready to hand your paper in
12. Answer all questions; guess unless instructed otherwise
13. Leave time for review

  b. Essay questions
1. Read each question carefully
2. Determine exactly what is wanted. Underline key words or phrases.
3. Decide on outline or paragraph answer
4. Include many different points and elements unless asked to develop any one or two points or elements
5. Show impartiality by giving pros and cons unless directed to select one side only
6. Make and write down any assumptions you find necessary to answer the questions
7. Watch your English, grammar, punctuation and choice of words
8. Time your answers; don't crowd material

8) Answering the essay question

Most essay questions can be answered by framing the specific response around several key words or ideas. Here are a few such key words or ideas:

M's: manpower, materials, methods, money, management
P's: purpose, program, policy, plan, procedure, practice, problems, pitfalls, personnel, public relations

  a. Six basic steps in handling problems:
1. Preliminary plan and background development
2. Collect information, data and facts
3. Analyze and interpret information, data and facts
4. Analyze and develop solutions as well as make recommendations
5. Prepare report and sell recommendations
6. Install recommendations and follow up effectiveness

  b. Pitfalls to avoid
1. *Taking things for granted* – A statement of the situation does not necessarily imply that each of the elements is necessarily true; for example, a complaint may be invalid and biased so that all that can be taken for granted is that a complaint has been registered

2. *Considering only one side of a situation* – Wherever possible, indicate several alternatives and then point out the reasons you selected the best one
3. *Failing to indicate follow up* – Whenever your answer indicates action on your part, make certain that you will take proper follow-up action to see how successful your recommendations, procedures or actions turn out to be
4. *Taking too long in answering any single question* – Remember to time your answers properly

IX. AFTER THE TEST

Scoring procedures differ in detail among civil service jurisdictions although the general principles are the same. Whether the papers are hand-scored or graded by machine we have described, they are nearly always graded by number. That is, the person who marks the paper knows only the number – never the name – of the applicant. Not until all the papers have been graded will they be matched with names. If other tests, such as training and experience or oral interview ratings have been given, scores will be combined. Different parts of the examination usually have different weights. For example, the written test might count 60 percent of the final grade, and a rating of training and experience 40 percent. In many jurisdictions, veterans will have a certain number of points added to their grades.

After the final grade has been determined, the names are placed in grade order and an eligible list is established. There are various methods for resolving ties between those who get the same final grade – probably the most common is to place first the name of the person whose application was received first. Job offers are made from the eligible list in the order the names appear on it. You will be notified of your grade and your rank as soon as all these computations have been made. This will be done as rapidly as possible.

People who are found to meet the requirements in the announcement are called "eligibles." Their names are put on a list of eligible candidates. An eligible's chances of getting a job depend on how high he stands on this list and how fast agencies are filling jobs from the list.

When a job is to be filled from a list of eligibles, the agency asks for the names of people on the list of eligibles for that job. When the civil service commission receives this request, it sends to the agency the names of the three people highest on this list. Or, if the job to be filled has specialized requirements, the office sends the agency the names of the top three persons who meet these requirements from the general list.

The appointing officer makes a choice from among the three people whose names were sent to him. If the selected person accepts the appointment, the names of the others are put back on the list to be considered for future openings.

That is the rule in hiring from all kinds of eligible lists, whether they are for typist, carpenter, chemist, or something else. For every vacancy, the appointing officer has his choice of any one of the top three eligibles on the list. This explains why the person whose name is on top of the list sometimes does not get an appointment when some of the persons lower on the list do. If the appointing officer chooses the second or third eligible, the No. 1 eligible does not get a job at once, but stays on the list until he is appointed or the list is terminated.

X. HOW TO PASS THE INTERVIEW TEST

The examination for which you applied requires an oral interview test. You have already taken the written test and you are now being called for the interview test – the final part of the formal examination.

You may think that it is not possible to prepare for an interview test and that there are no procedures to follow during an interview. Our purpose is to point out some things you can do in advance that will help you and some good rules to follow and pitfalls to avoid while you are being interviewed.

What is an interview supposed to test?

The written examination is designed to test the technical knowledge and competence of the candidate; the oral is designed to evaluate intangible qualities, not readily measured otherwise, and to establish a list showing the relative fitness of each candidate – as measured against his competitors – for the position sought. Scoring is not on the basis of "right" and "wrong," but on a sliding scale of values ranging from "not passable" to "outstanding." As a matter of fact, it is possible to achieve a relatively low score without a single "incorrect" answer because of evident weakness in the qualities being measured.

Occasionally, an examination may consist entirely of an oral test – either an individual or a group oral. In such cases, information is sought concerning the technical knowledges and abilities of the candidate, since there has been no written examination for this purpose. More commonly, however, an oral test is used to supplement a written examination.

Who conducts interviews?

The composition of oral boards varies among different jurisdictions. In nearly all, a representative of the personnel department serves as chairman. One of the members of the board may be a representative of the department in which the candidate would work. In some cases, "outside experts" are used, and, frequently, a businessman or some other representative of the general public is asked to serve. Labor and management or other special groups may be represented. The aim is to secure the services of experts in the appropriate field.

However the board is composed, it is a good idea (and not at all improper or unethical) to ascertain in advance of the interview who the members are and what groups they represent. When you are introduced to them, you will have some idea of their backgrounds and interests, and at least you will not stutter and stammer over their names.

What should be done before the interview?

While knowledge about the board members is useful and takes some of the surprise element out of the interview, there is other preparation which is more substantive. It *is* possible to prepare for an oral interview – in several ways:

1) Keep a copy of your application and review it carefully before the interview

This may be the only document before the oral board, and the starting point of the interview. Know what education and experience you have listed there, and the sequence and dates of all of it. Sometimes the board will ask you to review the highlights of your experience for them; you should not have to hem and haw doing it.

2) Study the class specification and the examination announcement

Usually, the oral board has one or both of these to guide them. The qualities, characteristics or knowledges required by the position sought are stated in these documents. They offer valuable clues as to the nature of the oral interview. For example, if the job involves supervisory responsibilities, the announcement will usually indicate that knowledge of modern supervisory methods and the qualifications of the candidate as a supervisor will be tested. If so, you can expect such questions, frequently in the form of a hypothetical situation which you are expected to solve. NEVER go into an oral without knowledge of the duties and responsibilities of the job you seek.

3) Think through each qualification required

Try to visualize the kind of questions you would ask if you were a board member. How well could you answer them? Try especially to appraise your own knowledge and background in each area, *measured against the job sought*, and identify any areas in which you are weak. Be critical and realistic – do not flatter yourself.

4) Do some general reading in areas in which you feel you may be weak

For example, if the job involves supervision and your past experience has NOT, some general reading in supervisory methods and practices, particularly in the field of human relations, might be useful. Do NOT study agency procedures or detailed manuals. The oral board will be testing your understanding and capacity, not your memory.

5) Get a good night's sleep and watch your general health and mental attitude

You will want a clear head at the interview. Take care of a cold or any other minor ailment, and of course, no hangovers.

What should be done on the day of the interview?

Now comes the day of the interview itself. Give yourself plenty of time to get there. Plan to arrive somewhat ahead of the scheduled time, particularly if your appointment is in the fore part of the day. If a previous candidate fails to appear, the board might be ready for you a bit early. By early afternoon an oral board is almost invariably behind schedule if there are many candidates, and you may have to wait. Take along a book or magazine to read, or your application to review, but leave any extraneous material in the waiting room when you go in for your interview. In any event, relax and compose yourself.

The matter of dress is important. The board is forming impressions about you – from your experience, your manners, your attitude, and your appearance. Give your personal appearance careful attention. Dress your best, but not your flashiest. Choose conservative, appropriate clothing, and be sure it is immaculate. This is a business interview, and your appearance should indicate that you regard it as such. Besides, being well groomed and properly dressed will help boost your confidence.

Sooner or later, someone will call your name and escort you into the interview room. *This is it.* From here on you are on your own. It is too late for any more preparation. But remember, you asked for this opportunity to prove your fitness, and you are here because your request was granted.

What happens when you go in?

The usual sequence of events will be as follows: The clerk (who is often the board stenographer) will introduce you to the chairman of the oral board, who will introduce you to the other members of the board. Acknowledge the introductions before you sit down. Do not be surprised if you find a microphone facing you or a stenotypist sitting by. Oral interviews are usually recorded in the event of an appeal or other review.

Usually the chairman of the board will open the interview by reviewing the highlights of your education and work experience from your application – primarily for the benefit of the other members of the board, as well as to get the material into the record. Do not interrupt or comment unless there is an error or significant misinterpretation; if that is the case, do not hesitate. But do not quibble about insignificant matters. Also, he will usually ask you some question about your education, experience or your present job – partly to get you to start talking and to establish the interviewing "rapport." He may start the actual questioning, or turn it over to one of the other members. Frequently, each member undertakes the questioning on a particular area, one in which he is perhaps most competent, so you can expect each member to participate in the examination. Because time is limited, you may also expect some rather abrupt switches in the direction the questioning takes, so do not be upset by it. Normally, a board member will not pursue a single line of questioning unless he discovers a particular strength or weakness.

After each member has participated, the chairman will usually ask whether any member has any further questions, then will ask you if you have anything you wish to add. Unless you are expecting this question, it may floor you. Worse, it may start you off on an extended, extemporaneous speech. The board is not usually seeking more information. The question is principally to offer you a last opportunity to present further qualifications or to indicate that you have nothing to add. So, if you feel that a significant qualification or characteristic has been overlooked, it is proper to point it out in a sentence or so. Do not compliment the board on the thoroughness of their examination – they have been sketchy, and you know it. If you wish, merely say, "No thank you, I have nothing further to add." This is a point where you can "talk yourself out" of a good impression or fail to present an important bit of information. Remember, *you close the interview yourself.*

The chairman will then say, "That is all, Mr. _____, thank you." Do not be startled; the interview is over, and quicker than you think. Thank him, gather your belongings and take your leave. Save your sigh of relief for the other side of the door.

How to put your best foot forward

Throughout this entire process, you may feel that the board individually and collectively is trying to pierce your defenses, seek out your hidden weaknesses and embarrass and confuse you. Actually, this is not true. They are obliged to make an appraisal of your qualifications for the job you are seeking, and they want to see you in your best light. Remember, they must interview all candidates and a non-cooperative candidate may become a failure in spite of their best efforts to bring out his qualifications. Here are 15 suggestions that will help you:

1) Be natural – Keep your attitude confident, not cocky

If you are not confident that you can do the job, do not expect the board to be. Do not apologize for your weaknesses, try to bring out your strong points. The board is interested in a positive, not negative, presentation. Cockiness will antagonize any board member and make him wonder if you are covering up a weakness by a false show of strength.

2) Get comfortable, but don't lounge or sprawl

Sit erectly but not stiffly. A careless posture may lead the board to conclude that you are careless in other things, or at least that you are not impressed by the importance of the occasion. Either conclusion is natural, even if incorrect. Do not fuss with your clothing, a pencil or an ashtray. Your hands may occasionally be useful to emphasize a point; do not let them become a point of distraction.

3) Do not wisecrack or make small talk

This is a serious situation, and your attitude should show that you consider it as such. Further, the time of the board is limited – they do not want to waste it, and neither should you.

4) Do not exaggerate your experience or abilities

In the first place, from information in the application or other interviews and sources, the board may know more about you than you think. Secondly, you probably will not get away with it. An experienced board is rather adept at spotting such a situation, so do not take the chance.

5) If you know a board member, do not make a point of it, yet do not hide it

Certainly you are not fooling him, and probably not the other members of the board. Do not try to take advantage of your acquaintanceship – it will probably do you little good.

6) Do not dominate the interview

Let the board do that. They will give you the clues – do not assume that you have to do all the talking. Realize that the board has a number of questions to ask you, and do not try to take up all the interview time by showing off your extensive knowledge of the answer to the first one.

7) Be attentive

You only have 20 minutes or so, and you should keep your attention at its sharpest throughout. When a member is addressing a problem or question to you, give him your undivided attention. Address your reply principally to him, but do not exclude the other board members.

8) Do not interrupt

A board member may be stating a problem for you to analyze. He will ask you a question when the time comes. Let him state the problem, and wait for the question.

9) Make sure you understand the question

Do not try to answer until you are sure what the question is. If it is not clear, restate it in your own words or ask the board member to clarify it for you. However, do not haggle about minor elements.

10) Reply promptly but not hastily

A common entry on oral board rating sheets is "candidate responded readily," or "candidate hesitated in replies." Respond as promptly and quickly as you can, but do not jump to a hasty, ill-considered answer.

11) Do not be peremptory in your answers

A brief answer is proper – but do not fire your answer back. That is a losing game from your point of view. The board member can probably ask questions much faster than you can answer them.

12) Do not try to create the answer you think the board member wants

He is interested in what kind of mind you have and how it works – not in playing games. Furthermore, he can usually spot this practice and will actually grade you down on it.

13) Do not switch sides in your reply merely to agree with a board member

Frequently, a member will take a contrary position merely to draw you out and to see if you are willing and able to defend your point of view. Do not start a debate, yet do not surrender a good position. If a position is worth taking, it is worth defending.

14) Do not be afraid to admit an error in judgment if you are shown to be wrong

The board knows that you are forced to reply without any opportunity for careful consideration. Your answer may be demonstrably wrong. If so, admit it and get on with the interview.

15) Do not dwell at length on your present job

The opening question may relate to your present assignment. Answer the question but do not go into an extended discussion. You are being examined for a *new* job, not your present one. As a matter of fact, try to phrase ALL your answers in terms of the job for which you are being examined.

Basis of Rating

Probably you will forget most of these "do's" and "don'ts" when you walk into the oral interview room. Even remembering them all will not ensure you a passing grade. Perhaps you did not have the qualifications in the first place. But remembering them will help you to put your best foot forward, without treading on the toes of the board members.

Rumor and popular opinion to the contrary notwithstanding, an oral board wants you to make the best appearance possible. They know you are under pressure – but they also want to see how you respond to it as a guide to what your reaction would be under the pressures of the job you seek. They will be influenced by the degree of poise you display, the personal traits you show and the manner in which you respond.

ABOUT THIS BOOK

This book contains tests divided into Examination Sections. Go through each test, answering every question in the margin. We have also attached a sample answer sheet at the back of the book that can be removed and used. At the end of each test look at the answer key and check your answers. On the ones you got wrong, look at the right answer choice and learn. Do not fill in the answers first. Do not memorize the questions and answers, but understand the answer and principles involved. On your test, the questions will likely be different from the samples. Questions are changed and new ones added. If you understand these past questions you should have success with any changes that arise. Tests may consist of several types of questions. We have additional books on each subject should more study be advisable or necessary for you. Finally, the more you study, the better prepared you will be. This book is intended to be the last thing you study before you walk into the examination room. Prior study of relevant texts is also recommended. NLC publishes some of these in our Fundamental Series. Knowledge and good sense are important factors in passing your exam. Good luck also helps. So now study this Passbook, absorb the material contained within and take that knowledge into the examination. Then do your best to pass that exam.

EXAMINATION SECTION

EXAMINATION SECTION

TEST 1

DIRECTIONS: Each question or incomplete statement is followed by several suggested answers or completions. Select the one that BEST answers the question or completes the statement. *PRINT THE LETTER OF THE CORRECT ANSWER IN THE SPACE AT THE RIGHT.*

Questions 1-5.

DIRECTIONS: Questions 1 through 5 are to be answered on the basis of the extracts from Federal income tax withholding and Social Security tax tables shown below. These tables indicate the amounts which must be withheld from the employee's salary by his employer for Federal income tax and for Social Security. They are based on weekly earnings.

INCOME TAX WITHHOLDING TABLE							
The wages are		And the number of withholding allowances is					
At Least	But Less Than	5	6	7	8	9	10 or More
		The amount of income tax to be withheld shall be					
$300	$320	$24.60	$19.00	$13.80	$ 8.60	$4.00	$ 0
320	340	28.80	22.80	17.40	12.20	7.00	2.80
340	360	33.00	27.00	21.00	15.80	10.60	5.60
360	380	37.20	31.20	25.20	19.40	14.20	9.00
380	400	41.40	34.40	29.40	23.40	17.80	12.60
400	420	45.60	39.60	33.60	27.60	21.40	16.20
420	440	49.80	43.80	37.80	31.80	25.60	19.80
440	460	54.00	48.00	42.00	36.00	29.80	23.80
460	480	58.20	52.20	46.20	40.20	34.00	38.00
480	500	62.40	46.40	40.40	44.40	38.20	32.20

SOCIAL SECURITY TABLE					
WAGES		Tax to be Withheld	WAGES		Tax to be Withheld
At Least	But Less Than		At Least	But Less Than	
$333.18	$333.52	$19.50	$336.60	$336.94	$19.70
333.52	333.86	19.52	336.94	337.28	19.72
333.86	334.20	19.54	337.28	337.62	19.74
334.20	334.54	19.56	337.62	337.96	19.76
334.54	334.88	19.58	337.96	338.30	19.78
334.88	335.22	19.60	338.30	338.64	19.80
335.22	335.56	19.62	338.64	338.98	19.82
335.56	335.90	19.64	338.98	339.32	19.84
335.90	336.24	19.66	339.32	339.66	19.86
336.24	336.60	19.68	339.66	340.00	19.88

1. If an employee has a weekly wage of $379.50 and claims 6 withholding allowances, the amount of income tax to be withheld is
   A. $27.00   B. $31.20   C. $35.40   D. $37.20

   1._____

2. An employee had wages of $335.60 for one week. With eight withholding allowances claimed, how much income tax will be withheld from his salary?
   A. $8.60   B. $12.00   C. $13.80   D. $17.40

   2._____

3. How much social security tax will an employee with weekly wages of $335.60 pay?
   A. $19.60   B. $19.62   C. $19.64   D. $19.66

   3._____

4. Mr. Wise earns $339.80 a week and claims seven withholding allowances. What is his take-home pay after income tax and social security tax are deducted?
   A. $300.32   B. $302.52   C. $319.92   D. $322.40

   4._____

5. If an employee pays $19.74 in social security tax and claims eight withholding allowances, the amount of income tax that should be withheld from his wages is
   A. $8.60   B. $12.20   C. $13.80   D. $15.80

   5._____

6. A fundamental rule of bookkeeping states that an individual's assets equal his liabilities plus his proprietorship (ASSETS = LIABILITIES – PROPRIETORSHIP). Which of the following statements logically follows from this rule?
   A. ASSETS = PROPRIETORSHIP – LIABILITIES
   B. LIABILITIES = ASSETS + PROPRIETORSHIP
   C. PROPRIETORSHIP = ASSETS – LIABILITIES
   D. PROPRIETORSHIP = LIABILITIES + ASSETS

   6._____

7. Mr. Martin's assets consist of the following:
   Cash on Hand: $5,233.74
   Furniture: $4,925.00
   Government Bonds: $5,500.00
   What are his TOTAL assets?
   A. $10,158.74 $10,425.00   C. $10,733.74   D. $15,658.74

   7._____

8. If Mr. Mitchell has $627.04 in his checking account and then writes three checks for $241.74, $13.24, and $101.97, what will be his new balance?
   A. $257.88   B. $269.08   C. $357.96   D. $368.96

   8._____

9. An employee's net pay is equal to his total earnings less all deductions. If an employee's total earnings in a pay period are $497.05, what is his NET pay if he has the following deductions: Federal income tax, $90.32; FICA: $28.74; State tax: $18.79; City tax: $7.25; Pension: $1.88?
   A. $351.17   B. $351.07   C. $350.17   D. $350.07

   9._____

10. A petty cash fund had an opening balance of $85.75 on December 1. 10.____
Expenditures of $23.00, $15.65, $5.23, $14.75, and $26.38 were made out of his fund during the first 14 days of the month. Then, on December 17, another $38.50 was added to the fund.
If additional expenditures of $17.18, $3.29, and $11.64 were made during the remainder of the month, what was the FINAL balance of the petty cash fund at the end of December?
   A. $6.93   B. $7.13   C. $46.51   D. $91.40

Questions 11-15.

DIRECTIONS: Questions 11 through 15 are to be answered on the basis of the following instructions.

The chart below is used by the loan division of a city retirement system for the following purposes: (1) to calculate the monthly payment a member must pay on an outstanding loan; (2) to calculate how much a member owes on an outstanding loan after he has made a number of payments.

To calculate the amount a member must pay each month in repaying his loan, look at Column II on the chart. You will notice that each entry in Column II corresponds to a number appearing under the *Months* column; for example, 1.004868 corresponds to 1 month, 0.503654 corresponds to 2 months, etc. To calculate the amount a member must pay each month, use the following procedure: multiply the amount of the load by the entry in Column II which corresponds to the number of months over which the load will be paid back. For example, if a loan of $200 is taken out for six months, multiply $200 by 0.169518, the entry in Column II which corresponds to six months.

In order to calculate the balance still owed on an outstanding loan, multiply the monthly payment by the number in Column I which corresponds to the number of monthly payments which remain to be paid on the loan. For example, if a member is supposed to pay $106.00 a month for twelve months, after seven payments, five monthly payments remain. To calculate the balance owed on the loan at this point, multiply the $106.00 monthly payment by 4.927807, the number in Column I that corresponds to five months.

Months	Column I	Column II
1	0.995156	1.004868
2	1.985491	0.503654
3	2.971029	0.336584
4	3.951793	0.253050
5	4.927807	0.202930
6	5.899092	0.169518
7	6.865673	0.145652
8	7.827572	0.127754
9	8.784811	0.113833
10	9.737414	0.102697
11	10.685402	0.093586
12	11.628798	0.085994
13	12.567624	0.079570
14	13.501902	0.074064
15	14.431655	0.069292

11. If Mr. Carson borrows $1,500 for eight months, how much will he have to pay back each month?
    A. $187.16   B. $191.63   C. $208.72   D. $218.65

12. If a member borrows $2,400 for one year, the amount he will have to pay back each month is
    A. $118.78   B. $196.18   C. $202.28   D. $206.38

13. Mr. Elliott borrowed $1,700 for a period of fifteen months. Each month he will have to pay back
    A. $117.80   B. $116.96   C. $107.79   D. $101.79

14. Mr. Aylward is paying back a thirteen-month loan at the rate of $173.13 a month.
    If he has already made six monthly payments, how much does he owe on the outstanding loan?
    A. $1,027.38   B. $1,178.75   C. $1,188.65   D. $1,898.85

15. A loan was taken out for 15 months, and the monthly payment was $104.75. After two monthly payments, how much was still owed on this load?
    A. $515.79   B. $863.89   C. $1,116.76   D. $1,316.46

16. The ABC Corporation had a gross income of $125,500.00 in 2015. Of this, it paid 60% for overhead.
    If the gross income for 2016 increased by $6,500 and the cost of overhead increased to 61% of gross income, how much more did it pay for overhead in 2016 than in 2015?
    A. $1,320   B. $5,220   C. $7,530   D. $8,052

17. After one year, Mr. Richards paid back a total of $1,695.00 as payment for   17.____
    a $1,500.00 loan. All the money paid over $1,500.00 was simple interest.
    The interest charge was MOST NEARLY
    A. 13%   B. 11%   C. 9%   D. 7%

18. A checking account has a balance of $253.36.   18.____
    If deposits of $36.95, $210.23, and $7.34 and withdrawals of $117.35, $23.37,
    and $15.98 are made, what is the NEW balance of the account?
    A. $155.54   B. $351.18   C. $364.58   D. $664.58

19. In 2015, the W Realty Company spent 27% of its income on rent.   19.____
    If it earned $97,254.00 in 2015, the amount it paid for rent was
    A. $26.258.58   B. $26,348.58   C. $27,248.58   D. $27,358.58

20. Six percent simple annual interest on $2,436.18 is MOST NEARLY   20.____
    A. $145.08   B. $145.17   c. $146.08   D. $146.17

21. Assume that the XYZ Company has $10,402.72 cash on hand.   21.____
    If it pays $699.83 of this for rent, the amount of cash on hand would be
    A. $9,792.89   B. $9,702.89   C. $9,692.89   D. $9,602.89

22. On January 31, Mr. Warren's checking account had a balance of $933.68.   22.____
    If he deposited $36.40 on February 2, $126.00 on February 9, and $90.02 on
    February 16 and wrote no checks during this period, what was the balance of his
    account on February 17?
    A. $680.26   B. $681.26   C. $1,186.10   D. $1,187.00

23. Multiplying a number by .75 is the same as   23.____
    A. multiplying it by 2/3   B. dividing it by 2/3
    C. multiplying it by 3/4   D. dividing it by 3/4

24. In City Agency A, 2/3 of the employees are enrolled in a retirement system.   24.____
    City Agency B has the same number of employees as Agency A, and 60% of
    these are enrolled in a retirement system.
    If Agency A has a total of 660 employees, how many MORE employees does it
    have enrolled in a retirement system than does Agency B?
    B. 36   B. 44   C. 56   D. 66

25. Net Worth is equal to Assets minus Liabilities.   25.____
    If, at the end of year, a textile company had assets of $98,695.83 and liabilities of
    $59,238.29, what was its net worth?
    A. $38,478.54   B. $38,488.64   C. $39,457.54   D. $48,557.54

KEY (CORRECT ANSWERS)

1.	B		11.	B
2.	B		12.	D
3.	C		13.	A
4.	B		14.	C
5.	B		15.	D
6.	C		16.	B
7.	D		17.	A
8.	B		18.	B
9.	D		19.	A
10.	B		20.	D

21. B
22. C
23. C
24. B
25. C

TEST 2

DIRECTIONS: Each question or incomplete statement is followed by several suggested answers or completions. Select the one that BEST answers the question or completes the statement. *PRINT THE LETTER OF THE CORRECT ANSWER IN THE SPACE AT THE RIGHT.*

Questions 1-10.

DIRECTIONS: Questions 1 through 10 below present the identification numbers, initials, and last names of employees enrolled in a city retirement system. You are to choose the option (A, B, C, or D) that has the IDENTICAL identification number, initials, and last name as those given in each question.

<u>Sample Question</u>
B145698 JL Jones
    A. B146798 JL Jones   B. B145698 JL Jonas
    C. P145698 JL Jones   D. B145698 JL Jones

The correct answer is D. Only Option D shows the identification number, initials, and last name exactly as they are in the sample question. Options A, B, and C have errors in the identification number or last name.

1. J297483 PL Robinson
   A. J294783 PL Robinson B. J297483 PL Robinson
   C. J297483 Pl Robinson D. J297843 PL Robinson

2. S497662 JG Schwartz
   B. S497662 JG Schwarz   B. S497762 JG Schwartz
   C. S497662 JG Schwartz D. S497663 JG Schwartz

3. G696436 LN Alberton
   A. G696436 LM Alberton B. G696436 LN Albertson
   C. G696346 LN Albertson D. G696436 LN Alberton

4. R774923 AD Aldrich
   A. R774923 AD Aldrich   B. R744923 AD Aldrich
   C. R774932 AP Aldrich   D. R774932 AD Allrich

5. N239638 RP Hrynyk
   A. N236938 PR Hrynyk   B. N236938 RP Hrynyk
   C. N239638 PR Hrynyk   D. N239638 Hrynyk

6. R156949 LT Carlson
   A. R156949 LT Carlton   B. R156494 LT Carlson
   C. R159649 LT Carlton   D. R156949 LT Carlson

7. T524697 MN Orenstein
   A. T524697 MN Orenstein B. T524967 MN Orinstein
   C. T524697 NM Ornstein D. T524967 NM Orenstein

8. L346239 JD Remsen
   A. L346239 JD Remson
   B. L364239 JD Remsen
   C. L346329 JD Remsen
   D. L346239 JD Remsen

8.____

9. P966438 SB Rieperson
   A. P996438 SB Rieperson
   B. P466438 SB Rieperson
   C. R996438 SB Rieperson
   D. P966438 SB Rieperson

9.____

10. D749382 CD Thompson
    A. P749382 CD Thompson
    B. D749832 CD Thomsonn
    C. D749382 CD Thompson
    D. D749823 CD Thomspon

10.____

Questions 11-20.

DIRECTIONS: Assume that each of the capital letters in the table below represents the name of an employee enrolled in the city's employees' personnel system. The number directly beneath the letter represents the agency for which the employee works, and the small letter directly beneath represents the code for the employee's account.

Name of Employee	L	O	T	Q	A	M	R	N	C
Agency	3	4	5	9	8	7	2	1	6
Account Code	r	f	b	i	d	t	g	e	n

In each of the following Questions 11 through 20, the agency code numbers and the account code letters in Columns 2 and 3 should correspond to the capital letters in Column 1 and should be in the same consecutive order. For each question, look at each column carefully and mark your answer as follows:

If there are one or more errors in Column 2 only, mark your answer A.
If there are one or more errors in Column 3 only, mark your answer B.
I there are one or more errors in Column 2 and one or more errors in Column 3, mark your answer C.
If there are NO errors in either column, mark your answer D.

Sample Question

Column 1	Column 2	Column 3
TQLMOC	583746	birtfn

In Column 2, the second agency code number (corresponding to letter Q) should be 9, not 8. Column 3 is coded correctly to Column 1. Since there is an error only in Column 2, the correct answer is A.

3 (#2)

	COLUMN 1	COLUMN 2	COLUMN 3	
11.	QLNRCA	931268	iregnd	11._____
12.	NRMOTC	127546	egftbn	12._____
13.	RCTALM	265837	gndbrt	13._____
14.	TAMLON	578341	bdtrfe	14._____
15.	ANTORM	815427	debigt	15._____
16.	MRALON	728341	tgdrfe	16._____
17.	CTNQRO	657924	ndeigf	17._____
18.	QMROTA	972458	itgfbd	18._____
19.	RQMCOL	297463	gitnfr	19._____
20.	NOMRTQ	147259	eftgbi	20._____

Questions 21-25.

DIRECTIONS: Questions 21 through 25 are to be answered SOLELY on the basis of the following passage.

The city may issue its own bonds or it may purchase bonds as an investment. Bonds may be issued in various denominations, and the face value of the bond is its par value. Before purchasing a bond, the investor desires to know the rate of income that the investment may yield in computing the yield on a bond, it is assumed that the investor will keep the bond until the date of maturity, except for callable bonds which are not considered in this passage. To compute exact yield is a complicated mathematical problem, and scientifically prepared tables are generally used to avoid such computation. However, the approximate yield can be computed much more easily. In computing approximate yield, the accrued interest on the date of purchase should be ignored because the buyer who pays accrued interest to the seller receives it again at the next interest date. Bonds bought at a premium (which cost more) yield a lower rate of income than the same bonds bought at par (face value), and bounds bought at a discount (which cost less) yield a higher rate of income than the same bonds bought at par.

21. An investor bought a $10,000 city bond paying 6% interest. 21._____
 Which of the following purchase prices would indicate that the bond was bought at a premium?
 A. $9,000   B. $9,400   C. $10,000   D. $10,600

22. During 2016, a particular $10,000 bond paying 7 ½% sold at fluctuating prices. 22._____
 Which of the following prices would indicate that the bond was bought at a discount?
 A. $9,800   B. $10,000   C. $10,200   D. $10,750

23. A certain group of bonds was sold in denominations of $5,000, $10,000, $20,000, and $50,000.
In the following list of four purchase prices, which one is MOST likely to represent a bond sold at par value?
   A. $10,500   B. $20,000   C. $22,000   D. $49,000

24. When computing the approximate yield on a bond, it is DESIRABLE to
   A. assume the bond was purchased at par
   B. consult scientifically prepared tables
   C. ignore accrued interest on the date of purchase
   D. wait until the bond reaches maturity

25. Which of the following is MOST likely to be an exception to the information provided in the above passage?
   Bonds
   A. purchased at a premium   B. sold at par
   C. sold before maturity   D. which are callable

KEY (CORRECT ANSWERS)

1.	B	11.	D
2.	C	12.	C
3.	D	13.	B
4.	A	14.	A
5.	D	15.	B
6.	D	16.	D
7.	A	17.	C
8.	D	18.	D
9.	D	19.	A
10.	C	20.	D

21. D
22. A
23. B
24. C
25. D

TEST 3

DIRECTIONS: Each question or incomplete statement is followed by several suggested answers or completions. Select the one that BEST answers the question or completes the statement. *PRINT THE LETTER OF THE CORRECT ANSWER IN THE SPACE AT THE RIGHT.*

Questions 1-6.

DIRECTIONS: Questions 1 through 6 consist of computations of addition, subtraction, multiplication, and division. For each question, do the computation indicated, and choose the correct answer from the four choices given.

1. ADD: 8936
         7821
         8953
         4297
         9785
         6579

   A. 45371   B. 45381   C. 46371   D. 46381

   1.____

2. SUBTRACT: 95,432
              67,596

   A. 27,836   B. 27,846   C. 27,936   D. 27,946

   2.____

3. MULTIPLY: 987
              867

   A. 854609   B. 854729   C. 855709   D. 855729

   3.____

4. DIVIDE: 59)321439.0

   A. 5438.1   B. 5447.1   C. 5448.1   D. 5457.1

   4.____

5. DIVIDE: .057)721

   A. 12,648.0   B. 12,648.1   C. 12,649.0   D. 12,649.1

   5.____

6. ADD: 1/2 + 5/7
   A. 1 3/14   B. 1 2/7   C. 1 5/14   D. 1 3/7

   6.____

7. If the total number of employees in one city agency increased from 1,927 to 2,006 during a certain year, the percentage increase in the number of employees for that year is MOST NEARLY
   A. 4%   B. 5%   C. 6%   D. 7%

   7.____

8. During a single fiscal year, which totaled 248 workdays, one account clerk verified 1,488 purchase vouchers.
Assuming a normal work week of five days, what is the average number of vouchers verified by the account clerk in a one-week period during this fiscal year?
A. 25 B. 30 C. 35 D. 40

8._____

9. If the city department of purchase bought 190 computers for $793.50 each and 208 computers for $839.90 each, the TOTAL price paid for these computers is
A. $315,813.00 B. $325,464.20
C. $334,279.20 D. $335,863.00

9._____

Questions 10-14.

DIRECTIONS: Questions 10 through 14 are to be answered SOLELY on the basis of the information given in the following paragraph.

Since discounts are in common use in the commercial world and apply to purchases made by government agencies as well as business firms, it is essential that individuals in both public and private employment who prepare bills, check invoices, prepare payment vouchers, or write checks to pay bills have an understanding of the terms used. These include cash or time discount, trade discount, and disconnect series. A cash or time discount offers a reduction in price to the buyer for the prompt payment of the bill and is usually expressed as a percentage with a time requirement, stated in days, within which the bill must be paid in order to earn the discount. An example would be 3/10, meaning a 3% discount may be applied to the bill if the payment is forwarded to the vendor within ten days. On an invoice, the cash discount terms are usually followed by the net terms, which is the time in days allowed for ordinary payment of the bill. Thus, 3/10, Net 30 means that full payment is expected in thirty days if the cash discount of 3% is not taken for having paid the bill within ten days. When the expression Terms Net Cash is listed on a bill, it means that no deduction for early payment is allowed. A trade discount is normally applied to list prices by a manufacturer to show the actual price to retailers so that they may know their cost and determine markups that will allow them to operate competitively and at a profit. A trade discount is applied by the seller to the list price and is independent of a cash or time discount. Discounts may also be used by manufacturers to adjust prices charged to retailers without changing list prices. This is usually done by series discounting and is expressed as a series of percentages. To compute a series discount, such as 40%, 20%, 10%, first apply the 40% discount to the list price, then apply the 20% discount to the remainder, and finally apply the 10% discount to the second remainder.

10. According to the above passage, trade discounts are
A. applied by the buyer
B. independent of cash discounts
C. restricted to cash sales
D. used to secure rapid payment of bills

10._____

11. According to the above passage, if the sales terms 5/10, Net 60 appear on a bill in the amount of $100 dated December 5, 2016 and the buyer submits his payment on December 15, 2016, his PROPER payment should be
A. $60 B. $90 C. $95 D. $100

11._____

12. According to the above passage, if a manufacturer gives a trade discount of 40% for an item with a list price of $250 and the terms are Net Cash, the price a retail merchant is required to pay for this item is 12._____
    A. $250 B. $210 C. $150 D. $100

13. According to the above passage, a series discount of 25%, 20%, 10% applied to a list price of $200 results in an ACTUAL price to the buyer of 13._____
    A. $88 B. $90 C. $108 D. $110

14. According to the above passage, if a manufacturer gives a trade discount of 50% and the terms are 6/10, Net 30, the cost to a retail merchant of an item with a list price of $500 and for which he takes the time discount is 14._____
    A. $220 B. $235 C. $240 D. $250

Questions 15-22.

DIRECTIONS: Questions 15 through 22 each show in Column I the information written on five cards (lettered j, k, l, m, n) which have to be filed. You are to choose the option (lettered A, B, C, or D) in Column II which BEST represents the proper order of filing according to the information, rules, and sample question given below.

A file card record is kept of the work assignments for all the employees in a certain bureau. On each card is the employee's name, the date of work assignment, and the work assignment code number. The cards are to be filed according to the following rules:

FIRST: File in alphabetical order according to employee's name.

SECOND: When two or more cards have the same employee's name, file according to the assignment date, beginning with the earliest date.

THIRD: When two or more cards have the same employee's name and the same date, file according to the work assignment number beginning with the lowest number.

Column II shows the cards arranged in four different orders. Pick the option (A, B, C, or D) in Column II which shows the correct arrangement of the cards according to th above filing rules.

SAMPLE QUESTION

Column I
j. Cluney 4/8/02 (486503)
k. Roster 5/10/01 (246611)
l. Altool 10/15/02 (711433)
m. Cluney 12/18/02 (527610)
n. Cluney 4/8/02 (486500)

Column II
A. k, l, m, j, n
B. k, n, j, l, m
C. l, k, j, m, n
D. l, n, j, m, k

4 (#3)

The correct way to file the cards is:
- l. Altool 10/15/02 (71143)
- n. Cluney 4/8/02 (486500)
- j. Cluney 4/8/02 (486503)
- m. Cluney 12/18/02 (527610)
- k. Roster 5/10/01 (246611)

The correct filing order is shown by the letters l, n, j, m, k. The answer to the sample question is the letter D, which appears in front of the letters l, n, j, m, k in Column II.

COLUMN I   COLUMN II

15. j. Smith 3/19/03 (662118)   A. j, m, l, n, k   15.____
     k. Turner 4/16/99 (481349)   B. j, l, n, m, k
     l. Terman 3/20/02 (210229)   C. k, n, m, l, j
     m. Smyth 3/20/02 (481359)   D. j, n, k, l, m
     n. Terry 5/11/01 (672128)

16. j. Ross 5/29/02 (396118)   A. l, m, k, n, j   16.____
     k. Rosner 5/29/02 (439281)   B. m, l, k, n, j
     l. Rose 7/19/02 (723456)   C. l, m, k, j, n
     m. Rosen 5/29/03 (829692)   D. m, l, j, n, k
     n. Ross 5/29/02 (399118)

17. j. Sherd 10/12/99 (552368)   A. n, m, k, j, l   17.____
     k. Snyder 11/12/99 (539286)   B. j, m, l, k, n
     l. Shindler 10/13/98 (426798)   C. m, k, n, j, l
     m. Scherld 10/12/99 (552386)   D. m, n, j, l, k
     n. Schneider 11/12/99 (798213)

18. j. Carter 1/16/02 (489636)   A. k, n, j, l, m   18.____
     k. Carson 2/16/01 (392671)   B. n, k, m, l, j
     l. Carter 1/16/01 (486936)   C. n, k, l, j, m
     m. Carton 3/15/00 (489639)   D. k, n, l, j, m
     n. Carson 2/16/01 (392617)

19. j. Thomas 3/18/99 (763182)   A. m, l, j, k, n   19.____
     k. Tompkins 3/19/00 (928439)   B. j, m, l, k, n
     l. Thomson 3/21/00 (763812)   C. j, l, n, m, k
     m. Thompson 3/18/99 (924893)   D. l, m, j, n, k
     n. Tompson 3/19/99 (928793)

20. j. Breit 8/10/03 (345612)   A. m, j, n, k, l   20.____
     k. Briet 5/21/00 (837543)   B. n, m, j, k, l
     l. Bright 9/18/99 (931827)   C. m, j, k, l, n
     m. Breit 3/7/98 (553984)   D. j, m, k, l, n
     n. Brent 6/14/04 (682731)

5 (#3)

COLUMN I   COLUMN II

21. j. Roberts 10/19/02 (581932)   A. n, k, l, m, j   21._____
     k. Rogers 8/9/00 (638763)   B. n, k, l, j, m
     l. Rogers 7/15/97 (105689)   C. k, n, l, m, j
     m. Robin 3/8/92 (287915)   D. j, m, k, n, l
     n. Rogers 4/2/04 (736921)

22. j. Hebert 4/28/02 (719468)   A. n, k, j, m, l   22._____
     k. Herbert 5/8/01 (938432)   B. j, l, n, k, m
     l. Helbert 9/23/04 (832912)   C. l, j, k, n, m
     m. Herbst 7/10/03 (648599)   D. l, j, n, k, m
     n. Herbert 5/8/01 (487627)

23. In order to pay its employees, the Convex Company obtained bills and coins   23._____
     in the following denominations:

Denomination	$20	$10	$5	$1	$.50	$.25	$.10	$.05	$.01
Number	317	122	38	73	69	47	39	25	36

     What was the TOTAL amount of cash obtained?
     A. $7,874.76   B. $7,878.00   C. $7,889.25   D. $7,924.35

24. H. Partridge receives a weekly gross salary (before deductions) of $596.25.   24._____
     Through weekly payroll deductions of $19.77, he is paying back a load he took
     from his pension fund.
     If other fixed weekly deductions amount to $184.14, how much pay would Mr.
     Partridge take home over a period of 33 weeks?
     A. $11,446.92   B. $12,375.69   C. $12,947.22   D. $19,676.25

25. Mr. Robertson is a city employee enrolled in a city retirement system. He has   25._____
     taken out a loan from the retirement fund and is paying it back at the rate of
     $14.90 every two weeks.
     In eighteen weeks, how much money will he have paid back on the loan?
     A. $268.20   B. $152.80   C. $124.10   D. $67.05

26. In 2015, the Iridor Book Company had the following expenses: rent, $6,500;   26._____
     overhead, $52,585; inventory, $35,700; and miscellaneous, $1,275.
     If all of these expenses went up 18% in 2016, what would they TOTAL in 2016?
     A. $17,290.80   B. $78,768.20   C. $96,060.00   D. $113,350.80

27. Ms. Ranier had a gross salary of $355.36, paid once every week.   27._____
     If the deductions from each paycheck are $62.72, $25.13, $6.29, and $1,27, how
     much money would Ms. Ranier take home in four weeks?
     A. $1,039.80   B. $1,421.44   C. $2,079.60   D. $2,842.88

28. Mr. Martin had a net income of $19,100 for the year. 28.____
If he spent 34% on rent and household expenses, 3% on house furnishings, 25% on clothes, and 36% on food, how much was left for savings and other expenses?
   A. $196.00   B. $382.00   C. $649.40   D. $1,960.00

29. Mr. Elsberg can pay back a loan of $1,800 from the city employees' retirement 29.____
system if he pays back $36.69 every two weeks for two full years.
At the end of the two years, how much more than the original $1,800 he borrowed will Mr. Elsberg have paid back?
   A. $53.94   B. $107.88   C. $190.79   D. $214.76

30. Mrs. Nusbaum is a city employee, receiving a gross salary (salary before 30.____
deductions) of $31,200. Every two weeks, the following deductions are taken out of her salary: Federal Income Tax, $243.96; FICA, $66.39; State Tax, $44.58; City Tax, $20.91; Health Insurance, $4.71.
If Mrs. Nusbaum's salary and deductions remained the same for a full calendar year, what would her NET salary (gross salary less deductions) be in that year?
   A. $9,894.30   B. $21,305.70   C. $28,118.25   D. $30,819.45

KEY (CORRECT ANSWERS)

1.	C	11.	C	21.	D
2.	A	12.	C	22.	B
3.	D	13.	C	33.	A
4.	C	14.	B	24.	C
5.	D	15.	A	25.	C
6.	A	16.	C	26.	D
7.	A	17.	D	27.	A
8.	B	18.	C	28.	B
9.	B	19.	B	29.	B
10.	B	20.	A	30.	B

EXAMINATION SECTION

TEST 1

DIRECTIONS: Each question or incomplete statement is followed by several suggested answers or completions. Select the one that BEST answers the question or completes the statement. *PRINT THE LETTER OF THE CORRECT ANSWER IN THE SPACE AT THE RIGHT.*

1. A multi-line telephone with buttons for eight separate lines, plus a *hold* button, is often used when an office requires more than one outside line.
   If you are talking on one line of this type of office phone when another call comes in, what is the procedure to follow if you want to answer the second call but keep the first call on the line?
   Push the
   A. *hold* button at the same time as you push the *pickup* button of the ringing line
   B. *hold* button and then push the *pickup* button of the ringing line
   C. *pickup* button of the ringing line and then push the *hold* button
   D. *pickup* button of the ringing line and push the *hold* button when you return to the original line

   1.____

2. Suppose that you are asked to prepare a petty cash statement for March. The original and one copy are to go to the personnel office. One copy is to go to the fiscal office, and another copy is to go to your supervisor. The last copy is for your files.
   In preparing the statement and the copies, how many sheets of copy paper should you use?
   A. 3   B. 4   C. 5   D. 8

   2.____

3. Which one of the following is the LEAST important advantage of putting the subject of a letter in the heading to the right of the address? It
   A. makes filing of the copy easier
   B. makes more space available in the body of the letter
   C. simplifies distribution of letters
   D. simplifies determination of the subject of the letter

   3.____

4. Of the following, the MOST efficient way to put 100 copies of a one-page letter into 9½" x 4⅛" envelopes for mailing is to fold _____ into an envelope.
   A. each letter and insert it immediately after folding
   B. each letter separately until all 100 are folded; then insert each one
   C. the 100 letters two at a time, then separate them and insert each one
   D. two letters together, slip them apart, and insert each one

   4.____

5. When preparing papers for filing, it is NOT desirable to　　5.____
   A. smooth papers that are wrinkled
   B. use paper clips to keep related papers together in the files
   C. arrange the papers in the order in which they will be filed
   D. mend torn papers with cellophane tape

6. Of the following, the BEST reason for a clerical unit to have its own duplicating　　6.____
   machine is that the unit
   A. uses many forms which it must reproduce internally
   B. must make two copies of each piece of incoming mail for a special file
   C. must make seven copies of each piece of outgoing mail
   D. must type 200 envelopes each month for distribution to the same offices

7. Several offices use the same photocopying machine.　　7.____
   If each office must pay its share of the cost of running this machine, the BEST
   way of determining how much of this cost should be charged to each of these
   offices is to
   A. determine the monthly number of photocopies made by each office
   B. determine the monthly number of originals submitted for photocopying by
      each office
   C. determine the number of times per day each office uses the photocopying
      machine
   D. divide the total cost of running the photocopy machine by the total
      number of offices using the machine

8. Which one of the following would it be BEST to use to indicate that a file folder　　8.____
   has been removed from the files for temporary use in another office?
   A(n)
   A. cross-reference card   B. tickler file marker
   C. aperture card   D. out guide

9. Which one of the following is the MOST important objective of filing?　　9.____
   A. Giving a secretary something to do in her spare time
   B. Making it possible to locate information quickly
   C. Providing a place to store unneeded documents
   D. Keeping extra papers from accumulating on workers' desks

10. If a check has been made out for an incorrect amount, the BEST action for　　10.____
    the writer of the check to take is to
    A. erase the original amount and enter the correct amount
    B. cross out the original amount with a single line and enter the correct
       amount above it
    C. black out the original amount so that it cannot be read and enter the
       correct amount above it
    D. write a new check

11. Which one of the following BEST describes the usual arrangement of a tickler file? 11.____
    A. Alphabetical   B. Chronological
    C. Numerical   D. Geographical

12. Which one of the following is the LEAST desirable filing practice? 12.____
    A. Using staples to keep papers together
    B. Filing all material without regard to date
    C. Keeping a record of all materials removed from the files
    D. Writing filing instructions on each paper prior to filing

13. Assume that one of your duties is to keep records of the office supplies used by your unit for the purpose of ordering new supplies when the old supplies run out. 13.____
    The information that will be of MOST help in letting you know when to reorder supplies is the
    A. quantity issued   B. quantity received
    C. quantity on hand   D. stock number

Questions 14-19.

DIRECTIONS: Questions 14 through 19 consist of sets of names and addresses. In each question, the name and address in Column II should be an exact copy of the name and address in Column I. If there is
a mistake *only* in the name, mark your answer A;
a mistake *only* in the address, mark your answer B;
a mistake in *both* name and address, mark your answer C;
no mistake in either name or address, mark your answer D.

SAMPLE QUESTION

Column I
Michael Filbert
456 Reade Street
New York, N.Y. 10013

Column II
Michael Filbert
645 Reade Street
New York, N.Y. 10013

Since there is a mistake only in the address (the street number should be 456 instead of 645), the answer to the sample question is B.

COLUMN I   COLUMN II

14. Esta Wong   Esta Wang   14.____
    141 West 68 St.   141 West 68 St.
    New York, N.Y. 10023   New York,, N.Y. 10023

15. Dr. Alberto Grosso   Dr. Alberto Grosso   15.____
    3475 12th Avenue   3475 12th Avenue
    Brooklyn, N.Y. 11218   Brooklyn, N.Y. 11218

	Column I	Column II	
16.	Mrs. Ruth Bortlas 482 Theresa Ct. Far Rockaway, N.Y. 11691	Ms. Ruth Bortlas 482 Theresa Ct. Far Rockaway, N.Y. 11169	16.____
17.	Mr. and Mrs. Howard Fox 2301 Sedgwick Avenue Bronx, N.Y. 10468	Mr. and Mrs. Howard Fox 231 Sedgwick Ave. Bronx, N.Y. 10458	17.____
18.	Miss Marjorie Black 223 East 23 Street New York, N.Y. 10010	Miss Margorie Black 223 East 23 Street New York, N.Y. 10010	18.____
19.	Michelle Herman 806 Valley Rd. Old Tappan, N.J. 07675	Michelle Hermann 806 Valley Dr. Old Tappan, N.J. 07675	19.____

Questions 20-25.

DIRECTIONS: Questions 20 through 25 are to be answered SOLELY on the basis of the information in the following passage.

Basic to every office is the need for proper lighting. Inadequate lighting is a familiar cause of fatigue and serves to create a somewhat dismal atmosphere in the office. One requirement of proper lighting is that it be of an appropriate intensity. Intensity is measured in foot-candles. According to the Illuminating Engineering Society of New York, for casual seeing tasks such as in reception rooms, inactive file rooms, and other service areas, it is recommended that the amount of light be 30 foot-candles. For ordinary seeing tasks such as reading and work in active file rooms and in mail rooms, the recommended lighting is 100 foot-candles. For very difficult seeing tasks such as accounting, transcribing, and business machine use, the recommended lighting is 150 foot-candles.

Lighting intensity is only one requirement. Shadows and glare are to be avoided. For example, the larger the proportion of a ceiling filled with lighting units, the more glare-free and comfortable the lighting will be. Natural lighting from windows is not too dependable because on dark wintry days, windows yield little usable light, and on sunny afternoons, the glare from windows may be very distracting. Desks should not face the windows. Finally, the main lighting source ought to be overhead and to the left of the user.

20. According to the above passage, insufficient light in the office may cause   20.____
    A. glare   B. shadows   C. tiredness   D. distraction

21. Based on the above passage, which of the following must be considered when   21.____
    planning lighting arrangements?
    The
      A. amount of natural light present
      B. amount of work to be done
      C. level of difficulty of work to be done
      D. type of activity to be carried out

22. It can be inferred from the above passage that a well-coordinated lighting scheme is LIKELY to result in
    A. greater employee productivity
    B. elimination of light reflection
    C. lower lighting cost
    D. more use of natural light

    22._____

23. Of the following, the BEST title for the above passage is
    A. Characteristics of Light
    B. Light Measurement Devices
    C. Factors to Consider When Planning Lighting Systems
    D. Comfort vs. Cost When Devising Lighting Arrangements

    23._____

24. According to the above passage, a foot-candle is a measurement of the
    A. number of bulbs used
    B. strength of the light
    C. contrast between glare and shadow
    D. proportion of the ceiling filled with lighting units

    24._____

25. According to the above passage, the number of foot-candles of light that would be needed to copy figures onto a payroll is _____ foot-candles.
    A. less than 30   B. 30   C. 100   D. 150

    25._____

KEY (CORRECT ANSWERS)

1.	B	11.	B
2.	B	12.	B
3.	B	13.	C
4.	A	14.	A
5.	B	15.	D
6.	A	16.	C
7.	A	17.	B
8.	D	18.	A
9.	B	19.	C
10.	D	20.	C

21. D
22. A
23. C
24. B
25. D

TEST 2

DIRECTIONS: Each question or incomplete statement is followed by several suggested answers or completions. Select the one that BEST answers the question or completes the statement. *PRINT THE LETTER OF THE CORRECT ANSWER IN THE SPACE AT THE RIGHT.*

1. Assume that a supervisor has three subordinates who perform clerical tasks. One of the employees retires and is replaced by someone who is transferred from another unit in the agency. The transferred employee tells the supervisor that she has worked as a clerical employee for two years and understands clerical operations quite well. The supervisor then assigns the transferred employee to a desk, tells the employee to begin working, and returns to his own desk.
The supervisor's action in this situation is
    A. *proper;* experienced clerical employees do not require training when they are transferred to new assignments
    B. *improper;* before the supervisor returns to his desk, he should tell the other two subordinates to watch the transferred employee perform the work
    C. *proper;* if the transferred employee makes any mistakes, she will bring them to the supervisor's attention
    D. *improper;* the supervisor should find out what clerical tasks the transferred employee has performed and give her instruction in those which are new or different

1.____

2. Assume that you are falling behind in completing your work assignments and you believe that your workload is too heavy.
Of the following, the BEST course of action for you to take FIRST is to
    A. discuss the problem with your supervisor
    B. decide which of your assignments can be postponed
    C. try to get some of your co-workers to help you out
    D. plan to take some of the work home with you in order to catch up

2.____

3. Suppose that one of the clerks under your supervision is filling in monthly personnel forms. She asks you to explain a particular personnel regulation which is related to various items on the forms. You are not thoroughly familiar with the regulation.
Of the following responses you may make, the one which will gain the MOST respect from the clerk and which is generally the MOST advisable is to
    A. tell the clerk to do the best she can and that you will check her work later
    B. inform the clerk that you are not sure of a correct explanation but suggest a procedure for her to follow
    C. give the clerk a suitable interpretation so that she will think you are familiar with all regulations
    D. tell the clerk that you will have to read the regulation more thoroughly before you can give her an explanation

3.____

4. Charging out records until a specified due date, with prompt follow-up if they are not returned, is a 4.____
   A. *good* idea; it may prevent the records from being kept needlessly on someone's desk for long periods of time
   B. *good* idea; it will indicate the extent of your authority to other departments
   C. *poor* idea; the person borrowing the material may make an error because of the pressure put upon him to return the records
   D. *poor* idea; other departments will feel that you do not trust them with the records and they will be resentful

Questions 5-9.

DIRECTIONS: Questions 5 through 9 consist of three lines of code letters and numbers. The numbers on each line should correspond with the code letters on the same line in accordance with the table below.

Code Letter	P	L	I	J	B	O	H	U	C	G
Corresponding Letter	0	1	2	3	4	5	6	7	8	9

On some of the lines, an error exists in the coding. Compare the letters and numbers in each question carefully. If you find an error or errors on
only one of the lines in the question, mark your answer A;
any two lines in the question, mark your answer B;
all three lines in the question, mark your answer C;
none of the lines in the question, mark your answer D.

SAMPLE QUESTION
JHOILCP   3652180
BICLGUP   4286970
UCIBHLJ   5824613

In the above sample, the first line is correct since each code letter listed has the correct corresponding number. On the second line, an error exists because code letter L should have the number 1 instead of the number 6. On the third line, an error exists because the code letter U should have the number 7 instead of the number 5. Since there are errors on two of the three lines, the correct answer is B.

5. BULJCIP   4713920 5.____
    HIGPOUL   6290571
    OCUHJJBI   5876342

6. CUBLOIJ   8741023 6.____
    LCLGCLB   1818914
    JPUHIOC   3076158

7. OIJGCBPO   52398405 7.____
    UHPBLIOP   76041250
    CLUIPGPC   81720908

8. BPCOUOJI   40875732   8._____
    UOHCIPLB   75682014
    GLHUUCBJ   92677843

9. HOIOHJLH   65256361   9._____
    IOJJHHBP   25536640
    OJHBJOPI   53642502

Questions 10-13.

DIRECTIONS: Questions 10 through 13 are to be answered SOLELY on the basis of the information given in the following passage.

The mental attitude of the employee toward safety is exceedingly important in preventing accidents. All efforts designed to keep safety on the employee's mind and to keep accident prevention a live subject in the office will help substantially in a safety program. Although it may seem strange, it is common for people to be careless. Therefore, safety education is a continuous process.

Safety rules should be explained, and the reasons for their rigid enforcement should be given to employees. Telling employees to be careful or giving similar general safety warnings and slogans is probably of little value. Employees should be informed of basic safety fundamentals. This can be done through staff meetings, informal suggestions to employees, movies, and safety instruction cards. Safety instruction cards provide the employees with specific suggestions about safety and serve as a series of timely reminder helping to keep safety on the minds of employees. Pictures, posters, and cartoon sketches on bulletin boards that are located in areas continually used by employees arouse the employees' interest in safety. It is usually good to supplement this type of safety promotion with intensive individual follow-up.

10. The above passage implies that the LEAST effective of the following safety   10._____
    measures is
       A. rigid enforcement of safety rules
       B. getting employees to think in terms of safety
       C. elimination of unsafe conditions in the office
       D. telling employees to stay alert at all times

11. The reason given by the passage for maintaining ongoing safety education is   11._____
    that
       A. people are often careless
       B. office tasks are often dangerous
       C. the value of safety slogans increases with repetition
       D. safety rules change frequently

12. Which one of the following safety aids is MOST likely to be preferred by the   12._____
    passage? A
       A. cartoon of a man tripping over a carton and yelling, *Keep aisles clear!*
       B. poster with a large number one and a caption saying, *Safety First*

24

C. photograph of a very neatly arranged office
D. large sign with the word *THINK* in capital letters

13. Of the following, the BEST title for the above passage is   13.____
    A. Basic Safety Fundamentals
    B. Enforcing Safety Among Careless Employees
    C. Attitudes Toward Safety
    D. Making Employees Aware of Safety

Questions 14-21.

DIRECTIONS: Questions 14 through 21 are to be answered SOLELY on the basis of the information and chart given below.

The following chart shows expenses in five selected categories for a one-year period, expressed as percentages of these same expenses during the previous year. The chart compares two different offices. In Office T (represented by ▓▓▓▓), a cost reduction program has been tested for the past year. The other office, Office Q (represented by ▨▨▨), served as a control, in that no special effort was made to reduce costs during the past year.

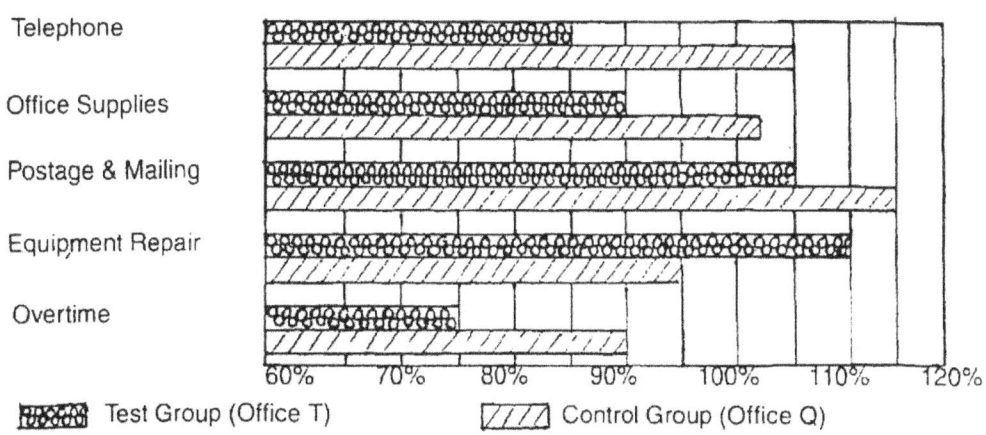

RESULTS OF OFFICE COST REDUCTION PROGRAM
Expenses of Test and Control Groups for 2020
Expressed as Percentages of Same Expenses for 2019

14. In Office T, which category of expense showed the greatest percentage   14.____
    REDUCTION from 2019 to 2020?
    A. Telephone   B. Office Supplies
    C. Postage & Mailing   D. Overtime

15. In which expense category did Office T show the BEST results in percentage   15.____
    terms when compared to Office Q?
    A. Telephone   B. Office Supplies
    C. Postage & Mailing   D. Overtime

16. According to the above chart, the cost reduction program was LEAST effective for the expense category of
    A. Office Supplies
    B. Postage & Mailing
    C. Equipment Repair
    D. Overtime

16._____

17. Office T's telephone costs went down during 2020 by approximately how many percentage points?
    A. 15
    B. 20
    C. 85
    D. 104

17._____

18. Which of the following changes occurred in expenses for Office Supplies in Office Q in the year 2020 as compared with the year 2019?
    They
    A. increased by more than 100%
    B. remained the same
    C. decreased by a few percentage points
    D. increased by a few percentage points

18._____

19. For which of the following expense categories do the results in Office T and the results in Office Q differ MOST NEARLYY by 10 percentage points?
    A. Telephone
    B. Postage & Mailing
    C. Equipment Repair
    D. Overtime

19._____

20. In which expense category did Office Q's costs show the GREATEST percentage increase in 2020?
    A. Telephone
    B. Office Supplies
    C. Postage & Mailing
    D. Equipment Repair

20._____

21. In Office T, by approximately what percentage did overtime expense change during the past year? It
    A. *increased* by 15%
    B. *increased* by 75%
    C. *decreased* by 10%
    D. *decreased* by 25%

21._____

22. In a particular agency, there were 160 accidents in 2017. Of these accidents, 75% were due to unsafe acts and the rest were due to unsafe conditions. In the following year, a special safety program was established. The number of accidents in 2019 due to unsafe acts was reduced to 35% of what it had been in 2017.
    How many accidents due to unsafe acts were there in 2019?
    A. 20
    B. 36
    C. 42
    D. 56

22._____

23. At the end of every month, the petty cash fund of Agency A is reimbursed for payments made from the fund during the month. During the month of February, the amounts paid from the fund were entered on receipts as follows: 10 bus fares of $3.50 each and one taxi fare of $35.00. At the end of the month, the money left in the fund was in the following denominations: 15 ten-dollar bills, 10 one-dollar bills, 40 quarters, and 100 dimes.
    If the petty cash fund is reduced by 20% for the following month, how much money will there be available in the petty cash fund for March?
    A. $110.00
    B. $200.00
    C. $215.00
    D. $250.00

23._____

24. The one of the following records which it would be MOST advisable to keep in alphabetical order is a
    A. continuous listing of phone messages, including time and caller, for your supervisor
    B. listing of individuals currently employed by your agency in a particular title
    C. record of purchases paid for by the petty cash fund
    D. dated record of employees who have borrowed material from the files in your office

25. Assume that you have been asked to copy by hand a column of numbers with two decimal places from one record to another. Each number consists of three, four, and five digits.
    In order to copy them quickly and accurately, you should copy
    A. each number exactly, making sure that the column of digits farthest to the right is in a straight line and all other columns are lined up
    B. the column of digits farthest to the right and then copy the next column of digits moving from right to left
    C. the column of digits farthest to the left and then copy the next column of digits moving from left to right
    D. the digits to the right of each decimal point and then copy the digits to the left of each decimal point

KEY (CORRECT ANSWERS)

1.	D	11.	A
2.	A	12.	A
3.	D	13.	D
4.	A	14.	D
5.	A	15.	A
6.	C	16.	C
7.	D	17.	A
8.	B	18.	D
9.	C	19.	B
10.	D	20.	C

21.	D
22.	C
23.	B
24.	B
25.	A

CLERICAL ABILITIES TEST
EXAMINATION SECTION
TEST 1

DIRECTIONS: Each question or incomplete statement is followed by several suggested answers or completions. Select the one that BEST answers the question or completes the statement. *PRINT THE LETTER OF THE CORRECT ANSWER IN THE SPACE AT THE RIGHT.*

Questions 1-10.

DIRECTIONS: Questions 1 through 10 consist of lines of names, dates, and numbers. For each question, you are to choose the option (A, B, C, or D) in Column II which EXACTLY matches the information in Column I. *PRINT THE LETTER OF THE CORRECT ANSWER IN THE SPACE AT THE RIGHT.*

SAMPLE QUESTION

Column I
Schneider 11/16/75 581932

Column II
A. Schneider 11/16/75 518932
B. Schneider 11/16/75 581932
C. Schnieder 11/16/75 581932
D. Shnieder 11/16/75 518932

The correct answer is B. Only Option B shows the name, date, and number exactly as they are in Column I. Option A has a mistake in the number. Option C has a mistake in the name. Option D has a mistake in the name and in the number. Now answer Questions 1 through 10 in the same manner.

	Column I	Column II	
1.	Johnston 12/26/74 659251	A. Johnson 12/23/74 659251 B. Johston 12/26/74 659251 C. Johnston 12/26/74 695251 D. Johnston 12/26/74 659251	1.____
2.	Allison 1/26/75 9939256	A. Allison 1/26/75 9939256 B. Alisson 1/26/75 9939256 C. Allison 1/26/76 9399256 D. Allison 1/26/75 9993356	2.____
3.	Farrell 2/12/75 361251	A. Farell 2/21/75 361251 B. Farrell 2/12/75 361251 C. Farrell 2/21/75 361251 D. Farrell 2/12/75 361151	3.____

4. Guerrero 4/28/72 105689
   A. Guererro 4/28/72 105689
   B. Guererro 4/28/72 105986
   C. Guererro 4/28/72 105869
   D. Guerrero 4/28/72 105689

   4.____

5. McDonnell 6/05/73 478215
   A. McDonnell 6/15/73 478215
   B. McDonnell 6/05/73 478215
   C. McDonnell 6/05/73 472815
   D. MacDonell 6/05/73 478215

   5.____

6. Shepard 3/31/71 075421
   A. Sheperd 3/31/71 075421
   B. Shepard 3/13/71 075421
   C. Shepard 3/31/71 075421
   D. Shepard 3/13/71 075241

   6.____

7. Russell 4/01/69 031429
   A. Russell 4/01/69 031429
   B. Russell 4/10/69 034129
   C. Russell 4/10/69 031429
   D. Russell 4/01/69 034129

   7.____

8. Phillips 10/16/68 961042
   A. Philipps 10/16/68 961042
   B. Phillips 10/16/68 960142
   C. Phillips 10/16/68 961042
   D. Philipps 10/16/68 916042

   8.____

9. Campbell 11/21/72 624856
   A. Campbell 11/21/72 624856
   B. Campbell 11/21/72 624586
   C. Campbell 11/21/72 624686
   D. Campbel 11/21/72 624856

   9.____

10. Patterson 9/18/71 76199176
    A. Patterson 9/18/72 76191976
    B. Patterson 9/18/71 76199176
    C. Patterson 9/18/72 76199176
    D. Patterson 9/18/71 76919176

    10.____

Questions 11-15.

DIRECTIONS: Questions 11 through 15 consist of groups of numbers and letters which you are to compare. For each question, you are to choose the option (A, B, C, or D) in Column I which EXACTLY matches the group of numbers and letters given in Column I.

SAMPLE QUESTION

Column I
B92466

Column II
A. B92644
B. B94266
C. A92466
D. B92466

The correct answer is D. Only Option D in Column II shows the group of numbers and letters EXACTLY as it appears in Column I. Now answer Questions 11 through 15 in the same manner.

Column I	Column II
11. 925AC5	A. 952CA5
	B. 925AC5
	C. 952AC5
	D. 925CA6

11.____

12. Y006925 | A. Y060925
 | B. Y006295
 | C. Y006529
 | D. Y006925

12.____

13. J236956 | A. J236956
 | B. J326965
 | C. J239656
 | D. J932656

13.____

14. AB6952 | A. AB6952
 | B. AB9625
 | C. AB9652
 | D. AB6925

14.____

15. X259361 | A. X529361
 | B. X259631
 | C. X523961
 | D. X259361

15.____

Questions 16-25.

DIRECTIONS: Each of questions 16 through 25 consists of three lines of code letters and three lines of numbers. The numbers on each line should correspond with the code letters on the same line in accordance with the table below.

Code Letter	S	V	W	A	Q	M	X	E	G	K
Corresponding Number	0	1	2	3	4	5	5	7	8	9

On some of the lines, an error exists in the coding. Compare the letters and numbers in each question carefully. If you find an error or errors on:
    only one of the lines in the question, mark your answer A;
    any two lines in the question, mark your answer B;
    all three lines in the question, mark your answer C;
    none of the lines in the question, mark your answer D.

SAMPLE QUESTION

WQGKSXG   2489068
XEKVQMA   6591453
KMAESXV   9527061

In the above sample, the first line is correct since each code letter listed has the correct corresponding number. On the second line, an error exists because code letter E should have the number 7 instead of the number 5. On the third line, an error exists because the code letter A should have the number 3 instead of the number 2. Since there are errors in two of the three lines, the correct answer is B. Now answer Questions 16 through 25 in the same manner.

16. SWQEKGA   0247983   16.____
     KEAVSXM   9731065
     SSAXGKQ   0036894

17. QAMKMVS   4259510   17.____
     MGGEASX   5897306
     KSWMKWS   9125920

18. WKXQWVE   2964217   18.____
     QKXXQVA   4966413
     AWMXGVS   3253810

19. GMMKASE   8559307   19.____
     AWVSKSW   3210902
     QAVSVGK   4310189

20. XGKQSMK   6894049   20.____
     QSVKEAS   4019730
     GSMXKMV   8057951

21. AEKMWSG   3195208   21.____
     MKQSVQK   5940149
     XGQAEVW   6843712

22. XGMKAVS   6858310   22.____
     SKMAWEQ   0953174
     GVMEQSA   8167403

23. VQSKAVE   1489317   23.____
     WQGKAEM   2489375
     MEGKAWQ   5689324

24. XMQVSKG   6541098   24.____
     QMEKEWS   4579720
     KMEVGKG   9571983

25. GKVAMEW   88912572   25.____
    AXMVKAE   3651937
    KWAGMAV   9238531

Questions 26-35.

DIRECTIONS: Each of Questions 26 through 35 consists of a column of figures. For each question, add the column of figures and choose the correct answer from the four choices given.

26. 5,665.43   26.____
    2,356.69
    6,447.24
    7,239.65

    A. 20,698.01   B. 21,709.01
    C. 21,718.01   D. 22,609.01

27. 817,209.55   27.____
    264,354.29
     82,368.76
    849,964.89

    A. 1,893.977.49   B. 1,989,988.39
    C. 2,009,077.39   D. 2,013,897.49

28. 156,366.89   28.____
    249,973.23
    823,229.49
     56,869.45

    A. 1,286,439.06   B. 1,287,521.06
    C. 1,297,539.06   D. 1,296,421.06

29. 23,422.15   29.____
    149,696.24
    238,377.53
     86,289.79
    505,533.63

    A. 989,229.34   B. 999,879.34
    C. 1,003,330.34   D. 1,023,329.34

30. 2,468,926.70
    656,842.28
    49,723.15
    832,369.59

    A. 3,218,062.72   B. 3,808,092.72
    C. 4,007,861.72   D. 4,818,192.72

31.   524,201.52
     7,775,678.51
     8,345,299.63
    40,628,898.08
    31,374,670.07

    A. 88,646,647.81   B. 88,646,747.91
    C. 88,648,647.91   D. 88,648,747.81

32. 6,824,829.40
      682,482.94
    5,542,015.27
      775,678.51
    7,732,507.25

    A. 21,557,513.37   B. 21,567,513.37
    C. 22,567,503.37   D. 22,567,513.37

33. 22,109,405.58
     6,097,093.43
     5,050,073.99
     8,118,050.05
     4,313,980.82

    A. 45,688,593.87   B. 45,688,603.87
    C. 45,689,593.87   D. 45,689,603.87

34. 79,324,114.19
    99,848,129.74
    43,331,653.31
    41,610,207.14

    A. 264,114,104.38   B. 264,114,114.38
    C. 265,114,114.38   D. 265,214,104.38

35. 33,729,653.94   35._____
     5,959,342.58
     26,052,715.47
     4,452,669.52
     7,079,953.59

     A. 76,374,334.10   B. 76,375,334.10
     C. 77,274,335.10   D. 77,275,335.10

Questions 36-40.

DIRECTIONS: Each of Questions 36 through 40 consists of a single number in Column I and four options in Column II. For each question, you are to choose the option (A, B, C, or D) in Column II which EXACTLY matches the number in Column I.

SAMPLE QUESTION

Column I   Column II
5965121   A. 5956121
                        B. 5965121
                        C. 5966121
                        D. 5965211

The correct answer is B. Only Option B shows the number EXACTLY as it appears in Column I. Now answer Questions 36 through 40 in the same manner.

Column I   Column II
36. 9643242   A. 9643242   36._____
                                          B. 9462342
                                          C. 9642442
                                          D. 9463242

37. 3572477   A. 3752477   37._____
                                          B. 3725477
                                          C. 3572477
                                          D. 3574277

38. 5276101   A. 5267101   38._____
                                          B. 5726011
                                          C. 5271601
                                          D. 5276101

39. 4469329   A. 4496329   39._____
                                          B. 4469329
                                          C. 4496239
                                          D. 4469239

40. 2326308	A. 2236308	40.____
B. 2233608
C. 2326308
D. 2323608

KEY (CORRECT ANSWERS)

1.	D	11.	B	21.	A	31.	D
2.	A	12.	D	22.	C	32.	A
3.	B	13.	A	23.	B	33.	B
4.	D	14.	A	24.	D	34.	A
5.	B	15.	D	25.	A	35.	C
6.	C	16.	D	26.	B	36.	A
7.	A	17.	C	27.	D	37.	C
8.	C	18.	A	28.	A	38.	D
9.	A	19.	D	29.	C	39.	B
10.	B	20.	B	30.	C	40.	C

TEST 2

DIRECTIONS: Each question or incomplete statement is followed by several suggested answers or completions. Select the one that BEST answers the question or completes the statement. *PRINT THE LETTER OF THE CORRECT ANSWER IN THE SPACE AT THE RIGHT.*

Questions 1-5.

DIRECTIONS: Each of Questions 1 through 5 consists of a name and a dollar amount. In each question, the name and dollar amount in Column II should be an EXACT copy of the name and dollar amount in Column I. If there is:
    a mistake only in the name, mark your answer A;
    a mistake only in the dollar amount, mark your answer B;
    a mistake in both the name and the dollar amount, mark your answer C;
    no mistake in either the name or the dollar amount, mark your answer D.

SAMPLE QUESTION

Column I	Column II
George Peterson	George Petersson
$125.50	$125.50

Compare the name and dollar amount in Column II with the name and dollar amount in Column I. The name *Petersson* in Column II is spelled *Peterson* in Column I. The amount is the same in both columns. Since there is a mistake only in the name, the answer to the sample question is A. Now answer Questions 1 through 5 in the same manner.

	Column I	Column II	
1.	Susanne Shultz $3440	Susanne Schultz $3440	1.____
2.	Anibal P. Contrucci $2121.61	Anibel P. Contrucci $2112.61	2.____
3.	Eugenio Mendoza $12.45	Eugenio Mendozza $12.45	3.____
4.	Maurice Gluckstadt $4297	Maurice Gluckstadt $4297	4.____
5.	John Pampellonne $4656.94	John Pammpellonne $4566.94	5.____

Questions 6-11.

DIRECTIONS: Each of Questions 6 through 11 consist of a set of names and addresses, which you are to compare. In each question, the name and addresses in Column II should be an EXACT copy of the name and address in Column I. If there is:
- a mistake only in the name, mark your answer A;
- a mistake only in the address, mark your answer B;
- a mistake in both the name and address, mark your answer C;
- no mistake in either the name or address, mark your answer D.

SAMPLE QUESTION

Column I	Column II
Michael Filbert	Michael Filbert
456 Reade Street	645 Reade Street
New York, N.Y. 10013	New York, N.Y. 10013

Since there is a mistake only in the address (the street number should be 456 instead of 645), the answer to the sample question is B. Now answer Questions 6 through 11 in the same manner.

	Column I	Column II	
6.	Hilda Goettelmann 55 Lenox Rd. Brooklyn, N.Y. 11226	Hilda Goettelman 55 Lenox Ave. Brooklyn, N.Y. 11226	6.____
7.	Arthur Sherman 2522 Batchelder St. Brooklyn, N.Y. 11235	Arthur Sharman 2522 Batcheder St. Brooklyn, N.Y. 11253	7.____
8.	Ralph Barnett 300 West 28 Street New York, New York 10001	Ralph Barnett 300 West 28 Street New York, New York 10001	8.____
9.	George Goodwin 135 Palmer Avenue Staten Island, New York 10302	George Godwin 135 Palmer Avenue Staten Island, New York 10302	9.____
10.	Alonso Ramirez 232 West 79 Street New York, N.Y. 10024	Alonso Ramirez 223 West 79 Street New York, N.Y. 10024	10.____
11.	Cynthia Graham 149-34 83 Street Howard Beach, N.Y. 11414	Cynthia Graham 149-35 83 Street Howard Beach, N.Y. 11414	11.____

Questions 12-20.

DIRECTIONS: Questions 12 through 20 are problems in subtraction. For each question do the subtraction and select your answer from the four choices given.

12. 232,921.85
    -179,587.68

    A. 52,433.17   B. 52,434.17
    C. 53,334.17   D. 53,343,17

    12._____

13. 5,531,876.29
    -3,897,158.36

    A. 1,634,717.93   B. 1,644,718.93
    C. 1,734,717.93   D. 1,7234,718.93

    13._____

14. 1,482,658.22
    -937,925.76

    A. 544,633.46   B. 544,732.46
    C. 545,632.46   D. 545,732.46

    14._____

15. 937,828.17
    -259,673.88

    A. 678,154.29   B. 679,154.29
    C. 688,155.39   D. 699,155.39

    15._____

16. 760,412.38
    -263,465.95

    A. 496,046.43   B. 496,946.43
    C. 496,956.43   D. 497,046.43

    16._____

17. 3,203,902.26
    -2,933,087.96

    A. 260,814.30   B. 269,824.30
    C. 270,814.30   D. 270,824.30

    17._____

18. 1,023,468.71
    -934,678.88

    A. 88,780.83   B. 88,789.83
    C. 88,880.83   D. 88,889.83

    18._____

19. 831,549.47
    -772,814.78

    A. 58,734.69   B. 58,834.69
    C. 59,735.69   D. 59,834.69

20. 6,306,181.74
    -3,617,376.99

    A. 2,687,904.99   B. 2,688,904.99
    C. 2,689,804.99   D. 2,799,905.99

Questions 21-30.

DIRECTIONS: Each of Questions 21 through 30 consists of three lines of code letters and three lines of numbers. The numbers on each line should correspond with the code letters on the same line in accordance with the table below.

Code Letter	J	U	B	T	Y	D	K	R	L	P
Corresponding Number	0	1	2	3	4	5	5	7	8	9

On some of the lines, an error exists in the coding. Compare the letters and numbers in each question carefully. If you find an error or errors on:
 only *one* of the lines in the question, mark your answer A;
 any *two* lines in the question, mark your answer B;
 all *three* lines in the question, mark your answer C;
 none of the lines in the question, mark your answer D.

SAMPLE QUESTION

   BJRPYUR   2079417
   DTBPYKJ   5328460
   YKLDBLT   4685283

In the above sample, the first line is correct since each code letter listed has the correct corresponding number. On the second line, an error exists because code letter P should have the number 9 instead of the number 8. The third line is correct since each code letter listed has the correct corresponding number. Since there is an error in *one* of the three lines, the correct answer is A. Now answer Questions 21 through 30 in the same manner.

21. BYPDTJL   2495308
    PLRDTJU   9815301
    DTJRYLK   5207486

22. RPBYRJK   7934706
    PKTYLBU   9624821
    KDLPJYR   6489047

23.	TPYBUJR	3942107	23._____
	BYRKPTU	2476931	
	DUKPYDL	5169458	
24.	KBYDLPL	6345898	24._____
	BLRKBRU	2876261	
	JTULDYB	0318542	
25.	LDPYDKR	8594567	25._____
	BDKDRJL	2565708	
	BDRPLUJ	2679810	
26.	PLRLBPU	9858291	26._____
	LPYKRDJ	88936750	
	TDKPDTR	3569527	
27.	RKURPBY	7617924	27._____
	RYUKPTJ	7426930	
	RTKPTJD	7369305	
28.	DYKPBJT	5469203	28._____
	KLPJBTL	6890238	
	TKPLBJP	3698209	
29.	BTPRJYL	2397148	29._____
	LDKUTYR	8561347	
	YDBLRPJ	4528190	
30.	ULPBKYT	1892643	30._____
	KPDTRBJ	6953720	
	YLKJPTB	4860932	

KEY (CORRECT ANSWERS)

1.	A	11.	D	21.	B
2.	C	12.	C	22.	C
3.	A	13.	A	23.	D
4.	D	14.	B	24.	B
5.	C	15.	A	25.	A
6.	C	16.	B	26.	C
7.	C	17.	C	27.	A
8.	D	18.	B	28.	D
9.	A	19.	A	29.	B
10.	B	20.	B	30.	D

NAME AND NUMBER COMPARISONS

COMMENTARY

This test seeks to measure your ability and disposition to do a job carefully and accurately, your attention to exactness and preciseness of detail, your alertness and versatility in discerning similarities and differences between things, and your power in systematically handling written language symbols.

It is actually a test of your ability to do academic and/or clerical work, using the basic elements of verbal (qualitative) and mathematical (quantitative) learning—words and numbers.

EXAMINATION SECTION

TEST 1

DIRECTIONS: In each line across the page there are three names or numbers that are much alike. Compare the three names or numbers and decide which ones are exactly alike. *PRINT IN THE SPACE AT THE RIGHT THE LETTER:*
A. if all THREE names or numbers are exactly alike
B. if only the FIRST and SECOND names or numbers are ALIKE
C. if only the FIRST and THIRD names or numbers are alike
D. if only the SECOND or THIRD names or numbers are alike
E. if ALL THREE names or numbers are DIFFERENT

1.	Davis Hazen	David Hozen	David Hazen	1._____
2.	Lois Appel	Lois Appel	Lois Apfel	2._____
3.	June Allan	Jane Allan	Jane Allan	3._____
4.	10235	10235	10235	4._____
5.	32614	32164	32614	5._____

TEST 2

1.	2395890	2395890	2395890	1._____
2.	1926341	1926347	1926314	2._____
3.	E. Owens McVey	E. Owen McVey	E. Owen McVay	3._____
4.	Emily Neal Rouse	Emily Neal Rowse	Emily Neal Rowse	4._____
5.	H. Merritt Audubon	H. Merriott Audubon	H. Merritt Audubon	5._____

TEST 3

1.	6219354	6219354	6219354	1.____
2.	231793	2312793	2312793	2.____
3.	1065407	1065407	1065047	3.____
4.	Francis Ransdell	Frances Ramsdell	Francis Ramsdell	4.____
5.	Cornelius Detwiler	Cornelius Detwiler	Cornelius Detwiler	5.____

TEST 4

1.	6452054	6452564	6542054	1.____
2.	8501268	8501268	8501286	2.____
3.	Ella Burk Newham	Ella Burk Newnham	Elena Burk Newnham	3.____
4.	Jno. K. Ravencroft	Jno. H. Ravencroft	Jno. H. Ravencoft	4.____
5.	Martin Wills Pullen	Martin Wills Pulen	Martin Wills Pullen	5.____

TEST 5

1.	3457988	3457986	3457986	1.____
2.	4695682	4695862	4695682	2.____
3.	Stricklund Kaneydy	Sticklund Kanedy	Stricklund Kanedy	3.____
4.	Joy Harlor Witner	Joy Harloe Witner	Joy Harloe Witner	4.____
5.	R.M.O. Uberroth	R.M.O. Uberroth	R.N.O. Uberroth	5.____

TEST 6

1.	1592514	1592574	1592574	1._____
2.	2010202	2010202	2010220	2._____
3.	6177396	6177936	6177396	3._____
4.	Drusilla S. Ridgeley	Drusilla S. Ridgeley	Drusilla S. Ridgeley	4._____
5.	Andrei I. Tooumantzev	Andrei I. Tourmantzev	Andrei I. Toumantzov	5._____

TEST 7

1.	5261383	5261383	5261338	1._____
2.	8125690	8126690	8125609	2._____
3.	W.E. Johnston	W.E. Johnson	W.E. Johnson	3._____
4.	Vergil L. Muller	Vergil L. Muller	Vergil L. Muller	4._____
5.	Atherton R. Warde	Asheton R. Warde	Atherton P. Warde	5._____

TEST 8

1.	013469.5	023469.5	02346.95	1._____
2.	33376	333766	333766	2._____
3.	Ling-Temco-Vought	Ling-Tenco-Vought	Ling-Temco Vought	3._____
4.	Lorilard Corp.	Lorillard Corp.	Lorrilard Corp.	4._____
5.	American Agronomics Corporation	American Agronomics Corporation	American Agronomic Corporation	5._____

TEST 9

1.	436592864	436592864	436592864	1.____
2.	197765123	197755123	197755123	2.____
3.	Dewaay Cortvriendt International S.A.	Deway Cortvriendt International S.A.	Deway Corturiendt International S.A.	3.____
4.	Crédit Lyonnais	Crèdit Lyonnais	Crèdit Lyonais	4.____
5.	Algemene Bank Nederland N.V.	Algamene Bank Nederland N.V.	Algemene Bank Naderland N.V.	5.____

TEST 10

1.	00032572	0.0032572	00032522	1.____
2.	399745	399745	398745	2.____
3.	Banca Privata Finanziaria S.p.A.	Banca Privata Finanzaria S.P.A.	Banca Privata Finanziaria S.P.A.	3.____
4.	Eastman Dillon, Union Securities & Co.	Eastman Dillon, Union Securities Co.	Eastman Dillon, Union Securities & Co.	4.____
5.	Arnhold and S. Bleichroeder, Inc.	Arnhold & S. Bleichroeder, Inc.	Arnold and S. Bleichroeder, Inc.	5.____

TEST 11

DIRECTIONS: Answer the questions below on the basis of the following instructions: For each such numbered set of names, addresses, and numbers listed in Columns I and II, select your answer from the following options:
- A. The names in Columns I and II are different
- B. The addresses in Columns I and II are different
- C. The numbers in Columns I and II are different
- D. The names, addresses and numbers are identical

1. Francis Jones
   62 Stately Avenue
   96-12446

   Francis Jones
   62 Stately Avenue
   96-21446

   1._____

2. Julio Montez
   19 Ponderosa Road
   56-73161

   Julio Montez
   19 Ponderosa Road
   56-71361

   2._____

3. Mary Mitchell
   2314 Melbourne Drive
   68-92172

   Mary Mitchell
   2314 Melbourne Drive
   68-92172

   3._____

4. Harry Patterson
   25 Dunne Street
   14-33430

   Harry Patterson
   25 Dunne Street
   14-34330

   4._____

5. Patrick Murphy
   171 West Hosmer Street
   93-81214

   Patrick Murphy
   171 West Hosmer Street
   93-18214

   5._____

TEST 12

1. August Schultz
   816 St. Clair Avenue
   53-40149

   August Schultz
   816 St. Claire Avenue
   53-40149

   1.____

2. George Taft
   72 Runnymede Street
   47-04033

   George Taft
   72 Runnymede Street
   47-04023

   2.____

3. Angus Henderson
   1418 Madison Street
   81-76375

   Angus Henderson
   1418 Madison Street
   81-76375

   3.____

4. Carolyn Mazur
   12 Rivenlew Road
   38-99615

   Carolyn Mazur
   12 Rivervane Road
   38-99615

   4.____

5. Adele Russell
   1725 Lansing Lane
   72-91962

   Adela Russell
   1725 Lansing Lane
   72-91962

   5.____

TEST 13

DIRECTIONS: The following questions are based on the instructions given below. In each of the following questions, the 3-line name and address in Column I is the master-list entry, and the 3-line entry in Column II is the information to be checked against the master list.
If there is one line that is NOT exactly alike, mark your answer A.
If there are two lines NOT exactly alike, mark your answer B.
If there are three lines NOT exactly alike, mark your answer C.
If the lines ALL are exactly alike, mark your answer D.

1. Jerome A. Jackson
   1243 14th Avenue
   New York, N.Y. 10023

   Jerome A. Johnson
   1234 14th Avenue
   New York, N.Y. 10023

   1.____

2. Sophie Strachtheim
   33-28 Connecticut Ave.
   Far Rockaway, N.Y. 11697

   Sophie Strachtheim
   33-28 Connecticut Ave.
   Far Rockaway, N.Y. 11697

   2.____

3. Elisabeth NT. Gorrell
   256 Exchange St
   New York, N.Y. 10013

   Elizabeth NT. Correll
   256 Exchange St.
   New York, N.Y. 10013

   3.____

4. Maria J. Gonzalez
   7516 E. Sheepshead Rd.
   Brooklyn, N.Y. 11240

   Maria J. Gonzalez
   7516 N. Shepshead Rd.
   Brooklyn, N.Y. 11240

   4.____

5. Leslie B. Brautenweiler
   21-57A Seller Terr.
   Flushing, N.Y. 11367

   Leslie B. Brautenwieler
   21-75ASeiler Terr.
   Flushing, N.J. 11367

   5.____

KEY (CORRECT ANSWERS)

TEST 1	TEST 2	TEST 3	TEST 4	TEST 5	TEST 6	TEST 7
1. E	1. A	1. A	1. E	1. D	1. D	1. B
2. B	2. E	2. A	2. B	2. C	2. B	2. E
3. D	3. E	3. B	3. E	3. E	3. C	3. D
4. A	4. D	4. E	4. E	4. D	4. A	4. A
5. C	5. C	5. A	5. C	5. B	5. E	5. E

TEST 8	TEST 9	TEST 10	TEST 11	TEST 12	TEST 13
1. E	1. A	1. E	1. C	1. B	1. B
2. D	2. D	2. B	2. C	2. C	2. D
3. E	3. E	3. E	3. D	3. D	3. A
4. E	4. E	4. C	4. C	4. B	4. A
5. B	5. E	5. E	5. C	5. A	5. C

NAME AND NUMBER CHECKING
EXAMINATION SECTION
TEST 1

DIRECTIONS: This test is designed to measure your speed/and accuracy. You are urged to work both quickly and accurately and to do correctly as many lists as you can in the time allowed. The test consists of lists or pairs of names and numbers. Count the number of IDENTICAL pairs in each list. Then, select the correct number, 1, 2, 3, 4, 5, and indicate your choice in the space at the right. Two sample questions are presented for your guidance, together with the correct solutions.

SAMPLE LIST A
Adelphi College	– Adelphia College
Braxton Corp	– Braxeton Corp.
Wassaic State School	– Wassaic State School
Central Islip State Hospital	– Central Isllip State Hospital
Greenwich House	– Greenwich House

NOTE: There are only two correct pairs—Wassaic State School and Greenwich House. Therefore, the CORRECT answer is 2.

SAMPLE LIST B
78453694	– 78453684
784530	– 784530
533	– 534
67845	– 67845
2368745	– 2368755

NOTE: There are only two correct pairs—784530 and 67845. Therefore, the CORRECT answer is 2.

LIST 1   1.____
98654327	- 98654327
74932564	- 7492564
61438652	- 61438652
01297653	- 01287653
1865439765	- 1865439765

LIST 2   2.____
478362	- 478363
278354792	- 278354772
9327	- 9327
297384625	- 27384625
6428156	- 6428158

LIST 3
- Abbey House — Abbey House
- Actor's Fund Home — Actor's Fund Home
- Adrian Memorial — Adrian Memorial
- A. Clayton Powell Home — Clayton Powell House
- Abbot E. Kittredge Club — Abbott E. Kitteredge Club

3.____

LIST 4
- 3682 — 3692
- 21937453829 — 31927453829
- 723 — 733
- 2763920 — 2763920
- 47293 — 47293

4.____

LIST 5
- Adra House — Adra House
- Adolescents' Court — Adolescents' Court
- Cliff Villa — Cliff Villa
- Clark Neighborhood House — Clark Neighborhood House
- Alma Mathews House — Alma Mathews House

5.____

LIST 6
- 28734291 — 28734271
- 63810263849 — 63810263846
- 26831027 — 26831027
- 368291 — 368291
- 7238102637 — 7238102637

6.____

LIST 7
- Albion State T.S. — Albion State T.C.
- Clara de Hirsch Home — Clara De Hirsch Home
- Alice Carrington Royce — Alice Carington Royce
- Alice Chopin Nursery — Alice Chapin Nursery
- Lighthouse Eye Clinic — Lighthouse Eye Clinic

7.____

LIST 8
- 327 — 329
- 712438291026 — 712438291026
- 2753829142 — 275382942
- 826287 — 826289
- 26435162839 — 26435162839

8.____

LIST 9
- Letchworth Village — Letchworth Village
- A.A.A.E. Inc. — A.A.A.E. Inc.
- Clear Pool Camp — Clear Pool Camp
- A.M.M.L.A. Inc. — A.M.M.L.A. Inc.
- J.G. Harbard — J.G. Harbord

9.____

3 (#1)

LIST 10
 8254 - 8256
 2641526 - 2641526
 4126389012 - 4126389102
 725 - 725
 76253917287 - 76253917287

10.____

LIST 11
 Attica State Prison - Attica State Prison
 Nellie Murrah - Nellie Murrah
 Club Marshall - Club Marshal
 Assissium Casea-Maria - Assissium Casa-Maria
 The Homestead - The Homestead

11.____

LIST 12
 2691 - 2691
 623819253627 - 623819253629
 28637 - 28937
 278392736 - 278392736
 52739 - 52739

12.____

LIST 13
 A.I.C.P. Boys Camp - A.I.C.P. Boy's Camp
 Einar Chrystie - Einar Christyie
 Astoria Center - Astoria Center
 G. Frederick Brown - G. Federick Browne
 Vacation Service - Vacation Services

13.____

LIST 14
 728352689 - 728352688
 643728 - 643728
 37829176 - 37827196
 8425367 - 8425369
 65382018 - 65382018

14.____

LIST 15
 E.S. Streim - E.S. Strim
 Charles E. Higgins - Charles E. Higgins
 Baluvelt, N.Y. - Blauwelt, N.Y.
 Roberta Magdalen - Roberto Magdalen
 Ballard School - Ballard School

15.____

LIST 16
 7382 - 7392
 281374538299 - 291374538299
 623 - 633
 6273730 - 6273730
 63392 - 63392

16.____

LIST 17   17.____
    Orrin Otis   - Orrin Otis
    Barat Settlement   - Barat Settlemen
    Emmanuel House   - Emmanuel House
    William T. McCreery   - William T. McCreery
    Seamen's Home   - Seaman's Home

LIST 18   18.____
    72824391   - 72834371
    3729106237   - 37291106237
    82620163849   - 82620163846
    37638921   - 37638921
    82631027   - 82631027

LIST 19   19.____
    Commonwealth Fund   - Commonwealth Fund
    Anne Johnsen   - Anne Johnson
    Bide-A-Wee Home   - Bide-a-Wee Home
    Riverdale-on-Hudson   - Riverdal-on-Hudson
    Bialystoker Home   - Bailystoker Home

LIST 20   20.____
    9271   - 9271
    392918352627   - 392018852629
    72637   - 72637
    927392736   - 927392736
    02739   - 92739

LIST 21   21.____
    Charles M. Stump   - Charles M. Stump
    Bourne Workshop   - Buorne Workshop
    B'nai Bi'rith   - B'nai Brith
    Poppenhuesen Institute - Poppenheusen Institute
    Consular Service   - Consular Service

LIST 22   22.____
    927352689   - 927352688
    647382   - 648382
    93729176   - 93727196
    649536718   - 649536718
    5835367   - 5835369

LIST 23   23.____
    L.S. Bestend   - L.S. Bestent
    Hirsch Mfg. Co.   - Hircsh Mfg. Co.
    F.H. Storrs   - F.P. Storrs
    Camp Wassaic   - Camp Wassaic
    George Ballingham   - George Ballingham

5 (#1)

LIST 24   24.____
   372846392048   - 372846392048
   334   - 334
   7283524678   - 7283524678
   7283   - 7283
   7283629372   - 7283629372

LIST 25   25.____
   Dr. Stiles Company   - Dr. Stills Company
   Frances Hunsdon   - Frances Hunsdon
   Northrop Barrert   - Nothrup Barrent
   J.D. Brunjes   - J.D. Brunjes
   Theo. Claudel & Co.   - Theo. Claudel co.

KEY (CORRECT ANSWERS)

1.	3	11.	3
2.	1	12.	3
3.	2	13.	1
4.	2	14.	2
5.	5	15.	2
6.	3	16.	2
7.	1	17.	3
8.	2	18.	2
9.	4	19.	2
10.	3	20.	4

21.	2
22.	1
23.	2
24.	5
25.	2

TEST 2

DIRECTIONS: This test is designed to measure your speed/and accuracy. You are urged to work both quickly and accurately and to do correctly as many lists as you can in the time allowed. The test consists of lists or pairs of names and numbers. Count the number of IDENTICAL pairs in each list. Then, select the correct number, 1, 2, 3, 4, 5, and indicate your choice in the space at the right.

LIST 1   1.____
    82728   - 82738
    82736292637   - 82736292639
    728   - 738
    83926192527   - 83726192529
    82736272   - 82736272

LIST 2   2.____
    L. Pietri   - L. Pietri
    Mathewson, L.F.   - Mathewson, L.F.
    Funk & Wagnall   - Funk & Wagnalls
    Shimizu, Sojio   - Shimizu, Sojio
    Filing Equipment Bureau   - Filing Equipment Buraeu

LIST 3   3.____
    63801829374   - 63801839474
    283577657   - 283577657
    65689   - 65689
    3457892026   - 3547893026
    2779   - 2778

LIST 4   4.____
    August Caille   - August Caille
    The Well-Fare Service - The Wel-Fare Service
    K.L.M. Process co.   - R.L.M. Process Co.
    Merrill Littell   - Merrill Littell
    Dodd & Sons   - Dodd & Son

LIST 5   5.____
    998745732   - 998745733
    723   - 723
    463849102983   - 463849102983
    8570   - 8570
    279012   - 279012

LIST 6   6.____
    M.A. Wender   - M.A. Winder
    Minneapolis Supply Co. - Minneapolis Supply Co.
    Beverly Hills Corp   - Beverley Hills Corp.
    Trafalgar Square   - Trafalgar Square
    Phifer, D.T.   - Phiefer, D.T.

2 (#2)

LIST 7   7._____
   7834629   - 7834629
   3549806746   - 3549806746
   97802564   - 97892564
   689246   - 688246
   2578024683   - 2578024683

LIST 8   8._____
   Scadrons'   - Scadrons'
   Gensen & Bro.   - Genson & Bro.
   Firestone Co.   - Firestone Co.
   H.L. Eklund   - H.L. Eklund
   Oleomargarine Co. - Oleomargarine Co.

LIST 9   9._____
   782039485618   - 782039485618
   53829172639   - 63829172639
   892   - 892
   82937482   - 829374820
   52937456   - 53937456

LIST 10   10._____
   First Nat'l Bank   - First Nat'l Bank
   Sedgwick Machine Works - Sedgewick Machine Works
   Hectographia Co.   - Hectographia Corp.
   Levet Bros.   - Levet Bros.
   Multistamp Co., Inc. - Multistamp Co., Inc.

LIST 11   11._____
   7293   - 7293
   6382910293   - 6382910292
   981928374012   - 981928374912
   58293   - 58393
   18203649271   - 283019283745

LIST 12   12._____
   Lowrey Lb'r Co.   - Lowrey Lb'r Co.
   Fidelity Service   - Fidelity Service
   Reumann, J.A.   - Reumann, J.A.
   Duophoto Ltd.   - Duophotos Ltd.
   John Jarratt   - John Jaratt

LIST 13   13._____
   6820384   - 6820384
   383019283745   - 383019283745
   63927102   - 63928102
   91029354829   - 91029354829
   58291728   - 58291728

LIST 14   14.____
    Standard Press Co.   - Standard Press Co.
    Reliant Mf'g. Co.   - Relant Mf'g Co.
    M.C. Lynn   - M.C. Lynn
    J. Fredericks Company   - G. Fredericks Company
    Wandermann, B.S.   - Wanderman, B.S.

LIST 15   15.____
    4283910293   - 4283010203
    992018273648   - 992018273848
    620   - 629
    752937273   - 752937373
    5392   - 5392

LIST 16   16.____
    Waldorf Hotel   - Waldorf Hotel
    Aaron Machinery Co.   - Aaron Machinery Co.
    Caroline Ann Locke   - Caroline Ane Locke
    McCabe Mfg. Co.   - McCabe Mfg. Co.
    R.L. Landres   - R.L. Landers

LIST 17   17.____
    68391028364   - 68391028394
    68293   - 68293
    739201   - 739201
    72839201   - 72839211
    739917   - 739719

LIST 18   18.____
    Balsam M.M.   - Balsamm, M.M.
    Steinway & Co.   - Stienway & M. Co.
    Eugene Elliott   - Eugene A. Elliott
    Leonard Loan Co.   - Leonard Loan Co.
    Frederick Morgan   - Frederick Morgen

LIST 19   19.____
    8929   - 9820
    392836472829   - 392836572829
    462   - 4622039271
    827   - 2039276837
    53829   - 54829

LIST 20   20.____
    Danielson's Hofbrau   - Danielson's Hafbrau
    Edward A. Truarme   - Edward A. Truame
    Insulite Co.   - Insulite Co.
    Reisler Shoe Corp.   - Rielser Shoe Corp.
    L.L. Thompson   - L.L. Thompson

4 (#2)

LIST 21   21.____
    92839102837   - 92839102837
    58891028   - 58891028
    7291728   - 7291928
    272839102839   - 272839102839
    428192   - 428102

LIST 22   22.____
    K.L. Veiller   - K.L. Veiller
    Webster, Roy   - Webster, Ray
    Drasner Spring Co.   - Drasner Spring Co.
    Edward J. Cravenport   - Edward J. Cravanport
    Harold Field   - Harold A. Field

LIST 23   23.____
    2293   - 2293
    4283910293   - 5382910292
    871928374012   - 871928374912
    68293   - 68393
    8120364927   - 81293649271

LIST 24   24.____
    Tappe, Inc   - Tappe, Inc.
    A.M. Wentingworth   - A.M. Wentinworth
    Scott A. Elliott   - Scott A. Elliott
    Echeverria Corp.   - Echeverria Corp.
    Bradford Victor Company - Bradford Victer Company

LIST 25   25.____
    4820384   - 4820384
    393019283745   - 283919283745
    63917102   - 63927102
    91029354829   - 91029354829
    48291728   - 48291728

KEY (CORRECT ANSWERS)

1.	1		11.	1
2.	3		12.	3
3.	2		13.	4
4.	2		14.	2
5.	4		15.	1
6.	2		16.	3
7.	3		17.	2
8.	4		18.	1
9.	2		19.	1
10.	3		20.	2

21.	3
22.	2
23.	1
24.	2
25.	4

ARITHMETIC

EXAMINATION SECTION
TEST 1

DIRECTIONS: Each question or incomplete statement is followed by several suggested answers or completions. Select the one that BEST answers the question or completes the statement. *PRINT THE LETTER OF THE CORRECT ANSWER IN THE SPACE AT THE RIGHT.*

1. From 30983 subtract 29998. The answer should be 1.____
    A. 985 B. 995 C. 1005 D. 1015

2. From $2537.75 subtract $1764.28. The answer should be 2.____
    A. $763.58 B. $773.47 C. $774.48 D. $873.58

3. From 254211 subtract 76348. The answer should be 3.____
    A. 177863 B. 177963 C. 187963 D. 188973

4. Divide 4025 by 35. The answer should be 4.____
    A. 105 B. 109 C. 115 D. 125

5. Multiply 0.35 by 2764. The answer should be 5.____
    A. 997.50 B. 967.40 C. 957.40 D. 834.40

6. Multiply 1367 by 0.50. The answer should be 6.____
    A. 6.8350 B. 68.350 C. 683.50 D. 6835.0

7. Multiply 841 by 0.01. The answer should be 7.____
    A. 0.841 B. 8.41 C. 84.1 D. 841

8. Multiply 1962 by 25. The answer should be 8.____
    A. 47740 B. 48460 C. 48950 D. 49050

9. Multiply 905 by 0.05. The answer should be 9.____
    A. 452.5 B. 45.25 C. 4.525 D. 0.4525

10. Multiply 8.93 by 4.7. The answer should be 10.____
    A. 41.971 B. 40.871 C. 4.1971 D. 4.0871

11. Multiply 25 by 763. The answer should be 11.____
    A. 18075 B. 18875 C. 19075 D. 20965

12. Multiply 2530 by 0.10. The answer should be 12.____
    A. 2.5300 B. 25.300 C. 253.00 D. 2530.0

13. Multiply 3053 by 0.25. The answer should be 13.____
   A. 76.325   B. 86.315   C. 763.25   D. 863.15

14. Multiply 6204 by 0.35. The answer should be 14.____
   A. 2282.40   B. 2171.40   C. 228.24   D. 217.14

15. Multiply $.35 by 7619. The answer should be 15.____
   A. $2324.75   B. $2565.65   C. $2666.65   D. $2756.75

16. Multiply 6513 by 45. The answer should be 16.____
   A. 293185   B. 293085   C. 292185   D. 270975

17. Multiply 3579 by 70. The answer should be 17.____
   A. 25053.0   B. 240530   C. 250530   D. 259530

18. A class had an average of 24 words correct on a spelling test. The class average on this spelling test was 80%. 18.____
   The AVERAGE number of words missed on this test was
   A. 2   B. 4   C. 6   D. 8

19. In which one of the following is 24 renamed as a product of primes? 19.____
   A. 2 x 6 x 2   B. 8 x 3 x 1
   C. 2 x 2 x 3 x 2   D. 3 x 4 x 2

Questions 20-23.

DIRECTIONS: In answering Questions 20 through 23, perform the indicated operation. Select the BEST answer from the choices below.

20. Add: 7068
          2807
          9434
          6179   20.____
   A. 26,488   B. 24,588   C. 25,488   D. 25,478

21. Divide: 75√45555   21.____
   A. 674   B. 607.4   C. 6074   D. 60.74

22. Multiply: 907
              x806   22.____
   A. 73,142   B. 13,202   C. 721,042   D. 731,042

23. Subtract: 60085
               -47194   23.____
   A. 12,891   B. 13,891   C. 12,991   D. 12,871

24. A librarian reported that 1/5% of all books taken out last school year had not been returned.
    If 85,000 books were borrowed from the library, how many were not returned?

    A.   170   B.   425   C.   1,700   D.   4,250

25. At 40 miles per hour, how many minutes would it take to travel 12 miles?

    A.   30   B.   18   C.   15   D.   20

KEY (CORRECT ANSWERS)

1. A		11. C
2. B		12. C
3. A		13. C
4. C		14. B
5. B		15. C
6. C		16. B
7. B		17. C
8. D		18. C
9. B		19. C
10. A		20. C

21. B
22. D
23. A
24. A
25. B

SOLUTIONS TO PROBLEMS

1. 30,983 - 29,998 = 985

2. $2537.75 - $1764.28 = $773.47

3. 254,211 - 76,348 = 177,863

4. 4025 ÷ 35 = 115

5. (.35)(2764) = 967.4

6. (1367)(.50) = 683.5

7. (841)(.01) = 8.41

8. (1962)(25) = 49,050

9. (905)(.05) = 45.25

10. (8.93)(4.7) = 41.971

11. (25)(763) = 19,075

12. (2530)(.10) = 253

13. (3053)(.25) = 763.25

14. (6204)(.35) = 2171.4

15. ($.35)(7619) = $2666.65

16. (6513)(45) = 293,085

17. (3579)(70) = 250,530

18. 24 ÷ .80 = 30. Then, 30 - 24 = 6 words

19. 24 = 2 x 2 x 3 x 2, where each number is a prime.

20. 7068 ÷ 2807 + 9434 + 6179 = 25,488

21. 45,555 ÷ 75 = 607.4

22. (907)(806) = 731,042

23. 60,085 - 47,194 = 12,891

24. (1/5%)(85,000) = (.002)(85,000) = 170 books

25. Let x = number of minutes. Then, $\dfrac{40}{60} = \dfrac{12}{x}$. Solving, x = 18

TEST 2

DIRECTIONS: Each question or incomplete statement is followed by several suggested answers or completions. Select the one that BEST answers the question or completes the statement. *PRINT THE LETTER OF THE CORRECT ANSWER IN THE SPACE AT THE RIGHT.*

1. The sum of 57901 + 34762 is 1._____
   A. 81663   B. 82663   C. 91663   D. 92663

2. The sum of 559 + 448 + 362 + 662 is 2._____
   A. 2121   B. 2031   C. 2021   D. 1931

3. The sum of 36153 + 28624 + 81379 is 3._____
   A. 136156   B. 146046   C. 146146   D. 146156

4. The sum of 742 + 9197 + 8972 is 4._____
   A. 19901   B. 18911   C. 18801   D. 17921

5. The sum of 7989 + 8759 + 2726 is 5._____
   A. 18455   B. 18475   C. 19464   D. 19474

6. The sum of $111.55 + $95.05 + $38.80 is 6._____
   A. $234.40   B. $235.30   C. $245.40   D. $254.50

7. The sum of 1302 + 46187 + 92610 + 4522 is 7._____
   A. 144621   B. 143511   C. 134621   D. 134521

8. The sum of 47953 + 58041 + 63022 + 22333 is 8._____
   A. 170248   B. 181349   C. 191349   D. 200359

9. The sum of 76563 + 43693 + 38521 + 50987 + 72723 is 9._____
   A. 271378   B. 282386   C. 282487   D. 292597

10. The sum of 85923 + 97211 + 11333 + 4412 + 22533 is 10._____
    A. 209302   B. 212422   C. 221412   D. 221533

11. The sum of 4299 + 54163 + 89765 + 1012 + 38962 is 11._____
    A. 188201   B. 188300   C. 188301   D. 189311

12. The sum of 48526 + 709 + 11534 + 80432 + 6096 is 12._____
    A. 135177   B. 139297   C. 147297   D. 149197

13. The sum of $407.62 + $109.01 + $68.44 + $378.68 is 13._____
    A. $963.75   B. $964.85   C. $973.65   D. $974.85

14. From 40614 subtract 4697. The answer should be   14._____

    A. 35917   B. 35927   C. 36023   D. 36027

15. From 81773 subtract 5717. The answer should be   15._____

    A. 75964   B. 76056   C. 76066   D. 76956

16. From $1755.35 subtract $1201.75. The answer should be   16._____

    A. $542.50   B. $544.50   C. $553.60   D. $554.60

17. From $2402.10 subtract $998.85. The answer should be   17._____

    A. $1514.35   B. $1504.25   C. $1413.25   D. $1403.25

18. Add: 12 1/2   18._____
             2 1/2
             3 1/2

    A. 17   B. 17 1/4   C. 17 3/4   D. 18

19. Subtract: 150   19._____
                -80

    A. 70   B. 80   C. 130   D. 150

20. After cleaning up some lots in the city dump, five cleanup crews loaded the following   20._____
    amounts of garbage on trucks:
        Crew No. 1 loaded 2 1/4 tons
        Crew No. 2 loaded 3 tons
        Crow No. 3 loadod 1 1/4 tons
        Crew No. 4 loaded 2 1/4 tons
        Crew No. 5 loaded 1/2 ton.
    The TOTAL number of tons of garbage loaded was

    A. 8 1/4   B. 8 3/4   C. 9   D. 9 1/4

21. Subtract: 17 3/4   21._____
                -7 1/4

    A. 7 1/2   B. 10 1/2   C. 14 1/4   D. 17 3/4

22. Yesterday, Tom and Bill each received 10 leaflets about rat control. They were supposed   22._____
    to distribute one leaflet to each supermarket in the neighborhood. When the day was
    over, Tom had 8 leaflets left. Bill had no leaflets left.
    How many supermarkets got leaflets yesterday?

    A. 8   B. 10   C. 12   D. 18

23. What is 2/3 of 1 1/8?   23._____

    A. 1 11/16   B. 3/4   C. 3/8   D. 4 1/3

24. A farmer bought a load of 120 bushels of corn.   24._____
    After he fed 45 bushels to his hogs, what fraction of his supply remained?

    A. 5/8   B. 3/5   C. 3/8   D. 4/7

25. In the numeral 3,159,217, the 2 is in the _____ column.   25.____

    A. hundreds   B. units   C. thousands   D. tens

KEY (CORRECT ANSWERS)

1.	D	11.	A
2.	B	12.	C
3.	D	13.	A
4.	B	14.	A
5.	D	15.	B
6.	C	16.	C
7.	A	17.	D
8.	C	18.	D
9.	C	19.	A
10.	C	20.	D

21. B
22. C
23. B
24. A
25. A

SOLUTIONS TO PROBLEMS

1. 57,901 + 34,762 = 92,663

2. 559 + 448 + 362 + 662 = 2031

3. 36,153 + 28,624 + 81,379 = 146,156

4. 742 + 9197 + 8972 = 18,911

5. 7989 + 8759 + 2726 = 19,474

6. $111.55 + $95.05 + $38.80 = $245.40

7. 1302 + 46,187 + 92,610 + 4522 = 144,621

8. 47,953 + 58,041 + 63,022 + 22,333 = 191,349

9. 76,563 + 45,693 + 38,521 + 50,987 + 72,723 = 282,487

10. 85,923 + 97,211 + 11,333 + 4412 + 22,533 = 221,412

11. 4299 + 54,163 + 89,765 + 1012 + 38,962 = 188,201

12. 48,526 + 709 + 11,534 + 80,432 + 6096 = 147,297

13. $407.62 + $109.01 + $68.44 + $378.68 = $963.75

14. 40,614 - 4697 = 35,917

15. 81,773 - 5717 = 76,056

16. $1755.35 - $1201.75 = $553.60

17. $2402.10 - $998.85 = $1403.25

18. 12 1/2 + 2 1/4 + 3 1/4 = 17 4/4 = 18

19. 150 - 80 = 70

20. 2 1/4 + 3 + 1 1/4 + 2 1/4 + 1/2 = 8 5/4 = 9 1/4 tons

21. 17 3/4 - 7 1/4 = 10 2/4 = 10 1/2

22. 10 + 10 - 8 - 0 = 12 supermarkets

23. $(\frac{2}{3})(1\frac{1}{8}) = (\frac{2}{3})(\frac{9}{8}) = \frac{18}{24} = \frac{3}{4}$

24. 120 - 45 = 75. Then, $\frac{75}{120} = \frac{5}{8}$

25. The number 2 is in the hundreds column of 3,159,217

TEST 3

DIRECTIONS: Each question or incomplete statement is followed by several suggested answers or completions. Select the one that BEST answers the question or completes the statement. *PRINT THE LETTER OF THE CORRECT ANSWER IN THE SPACE AT THE RIGHT.*

1. The distance covered in three minutes by a subway train traveling at 30 mph is _____ mile(s). 1._____

   A. 3 B. 2 C. 1 1/2 D. 1

2. A crate contains 3 pieces of equipment weighing 73, 84, and 47 pounds, respectively. 2._____
   The empty crate weighs 16 pounds.
   If the crate is lifted by 4 trackmen, each trackman lifting one corner of the crate, the AVERAGE number of pounds lifted by each of the trackmen is

   A. 68 B. 61 C. 55 D. 51

3. The weight per foot of a length of square-bar 4" x 4" in cross-section, as compared with one 2" x 2" in cross-section, is _____ as much. 3._____

   A. twice B. 2 1/2 times
   C. 3 times D. 4 times

4. An order for 360 feet of 2" x 8" lumber is shipped in 20-foot lengths. 4._____
   The MAXIMUM number of 9-foot pieces that can be cut from this shipment is

   A. 54 B. 40 C. 36 D. 18

5. If a trackman gets $10.40 per hour and time and one-half for working over 40 hours, his gross salary for a week in which he worked 44 hours should be 5._____

   A. $457.60 B. $478.40 C. $499.20 D. $514.80

6. If a section of ballast 6'-0" wide, 8'-0" long, and 2'-6" deep is excavated, the amount of ballast removed is _____ cu. feet. 6._____

   A. 96 B. 104 C. 120 D. 144

7. The sum of 7'2 3/4", 0'-2 7/8", 3'-0", 4'-6 3/8", and 1'-9 1/4" is 7._____

   A. 16'-8 1/4" B. 16'-8 3/4" C. 16'-9 1/4" D. 16'-9 3/4"

8. The sum of 3 1/16", 4 1/4", 2 5/8", and 5 7/16" is 8._____

   A. 15 3/16" B. 15 1/4" C. 15 3/8" D. 15 1/2"

9. Add: $51.79, $29.39, and $8.98. 9._____
   The CORRECT answer is

   A. $78.97 B. $88.96 C. $89.06 D. $90.16

10. Add: $72.07 and $31.54. Then subtract $25.75. 10._____
    The CORRECT answer is

    A. $77.86 B. $82.14 C. $88.96 D. $129.36

11. Start with $82.47. Then subtract $25.50, $4.75, and 35¢. 11.____
    The CORRECT answer is

    A. $30.60   B. $51.87   C. $52.22   D. $65.25

12. Add: $19.35 and $37.75. Then subtract $9.90 and $19.80. 12.____
    The CORRECT answer is

    A. $27.40   B. $37.00   C. $37.30   D. $47.20

13. Add: $153   13.____
             114
             210
            +186

    A. $657   B. $663   C. $713   D. $757

14. Add: $64.91   14.____
            13.53
            19.27
            20.00
           +72.84

    A. $170.25   B. $178.35   C. $180.45   D. $190.55

15. Add: 1963   15.____
            1742
           +2497

    A. 6202   B. 6022   C. 5212   D. 5102

16. Add: 206   16.____
            709
            1342
           +2076

    A. 3432   B. 3443   C. 4312   D. 4333

17. Subtract: $190.76   17.____
              -     .99

    A. $189.97   B. $189.87   C. $189.77   D. $189.67

18. From 99876 subtract 85397. The answer should be   18.____

    A. 14589   B. 14521   C. 14479   D. 13589

19. From $876.51 subtract $92.89. The answer should be   19.____

    A. $773.52   B. $774.72   C. $783.62   D. $784.72

20. From 70935 subtract 49489. The answer should be   20.____

    A. 20436   B. 21446   C. 21536   D. 21546

21. From $391.55 subtract $273.45. The answer should be 21._____
    A. $118.10   B. $128.20   C. $178.10   D. $218.20

22. When 119 is subtracted from the sum of 2016 + 1634, the answer is 22._____
    A. 2460   B. 3531   C. 3650   D. 3769

23. Multiply 35 x 65 x 15. The answer should be 23._____
    A. 2275   B. 24265   C. 31145   D. 34125

24. Multiply: 4.06 24._____
                x.031
    A. 1.2586   B. .12586   C. .02586   D. .1786

25. When 65 is added to the result of 14 multiplied by 13, the answer is 25._____
    A. 92   B. 182   C. 247   D. 16055

KEY (CORRECT ANSWERS)

1. C   11. B
2. C   12. A
3. D   13. B
4. C   14. D
5. B   15. A

6. C   16. D
7. C   17. C
8. C   18. C
9. D   19. C
10. A   20. B

21. A
22. B
23. D
24. B
25. C

SOLUTIONS TO PROBLEMS

1. Let x = distance. Then, $\frac{30}{60} = \frac{x}{3}$ Solving, x = 1 1/2 miles

2. (73 + 84 + 47 + 16) ÷ 4 = 55 pounds

3. (4 x 4) ÷ (2 x 2) = a ratio of 4 to 1.

4. 20 ÷ 9 = 2 2/9, rounded down to 2 pieces. Then, (360 ÷ 20)(2) = 36

5. Salary =($10.40)(40) + ($15.60)(4) = $478.40

6. (6)(8)(2 1/2) = 120 cu.ft.

7. $7'2\frac{3}{4}" + 0'2\frac{7}{8}" + 3'0" + 4'6\frac{3}{8}" + 1'9\frac{1}{4}" = 15'19\frac{18}{8}" = 15'21\frac{1}{4}" = 16'9\frac{1}{4}"$

8. $3\frac{1}{16}" + 4\frac{1}{4}" + 2\frac{5}{8}" + 5\frac{7}{16}" = 14\frac{22}{16}" = 15\frac{3}{8}"$

9. $51.79 + $29.39 + $8.98 = $90.16

10. $72.07 + $31.54 = $103.61. Then, $103.61 - $25.75 = $77.86

11. $82.47 - $25.50 - $4.75 - $0.35 = $51.87

12. $19.35 + $37.75 = $57.10. Then, $57.10 - $9.90 - $19.80 = $27.40

13. $153 + $114 + $210 + $186 = $663

14. $64.91 + $13.53 + $19.27 + $20.00 + $72.84 = $190.55

15. 1963 + 1742 + 2497 = 6202

16. 206 + 709 + 1342 + 2076 = 4333

17. $190.76 - .99 = $189.77

18. 99,876 - 85,397 = 14,479

19. $876.51 - $92.89 = $783.62

20. 70,935 - 49,489 = 21,446

21. $391.55 - $273.45 = $118.10

22. (2016 + 1634) - 119 = 3650 - 119 = 3531

23. (35)(65)(15) = 34,125

24. (4.06)(.031) = .12586

25. 65 + (14)(13) = 65 + 182 = 247

ARITHMETIC
EXAMINATION SECTION

DIRECTIONS: Each question or incomplete statement is followed by several suggested answers or completions. Select the one that BEST answers the question or completes the statement. *PRINT THE LETTER OF THE CORRECT ANSWER IN THE SPACE AT THE RIGHT.*

1. The sum of 53632 + 27403 + 98765 + 75424 is
    A. 19214   B. 215214   C. 235224   D. 255224

2. The sum of 76342 + 49050 + 21206 + 59989 is
    A. 196586   B. 206087   C. 206587   D. 234487

3. The sum of $452.13 + $963.45 + $621.25 is
    A. $1936.83   B. $2036.83   C. $2095.73   D. $2135.73

4. The sum of 36392 + 42156 + 98765 is
    A. 167214   B. 177203   C. 177313   D. 178213

5. The sum of 40125 + 87123 + 24689 is
    A. 141827   B. 151827   C. 151937   D. 161947

6. The sum of 2379 + 4015 + 6521 + 9986 is
    A. 22901   B. 22819   C. 21801   D. 21791

7. From 50962 subtract 36197.
   The answer should be
    A. 14675   B. 14765   C. 14865   D. 24765

8. From 90000 subtract 31928.
   The answer should be
    A. 58072   B. 59062   C. 68172   D. 69182

9. From 63764 subtract 21548.
   The answer should be
    A. 42216   B. 43122   C. 45126   D. 85312

10. From $9605.13 subtract $2715.96.
    The answer should be
    A. $12,321.09   B. $8,690.16   C. $6,990.07   D. $6,889.17

11. From 76421 subtract 73101.
    The answer should be
    A. 3642   B. 3540   C. 3320   D. 3242

12. From $8.25 subtract $6.50.
    The answer should be

    A. $1.25   B. $1.50   C. $1.75   D. $2.25

13. Multiply 563 by 0.50.
    The answer should be

    A. 281.50   B. 28.15   C. 2.815   D. 0.2815

14. Multiply 0.35 by 1045.
    The answer should be

    A. 0.36575   B. 3.6575   C. 36.575   D. 365.75

15. Multiply 25 by 2513.
    The answer should be

    A. 62825   B. 62725   C. 60825   D. 52825

16. Multiply 423 by 0.01.
    The answer should be

    A. 0.0423   B. 0.423   C. 4.23   D. 42.3

17. Multiply 6.70 by 3.2.
    The answer should be

    A. 2.1440   B. 21.440   C. 214.40   D. 2144.0

18. Multiply 630 by 517.
    The answer should be

    A. 325,710   B. 345,720   C. 362,425   D. 385,660

19. Multiply 35 by 846.
    The answer should be

    A. 4050   B. 9450   C. 18740   D. 29610

20. Multiply 823 by 0.05.
    The answer should be

    A. 0.4115   B. 4.115   C. 41.15   D. 411.50

21. Multiply 1690 by 0.10.
    The answer should be

    A. 0.169   B. 1.69   C. 16.90   D. 169.0

22. Divide 2765 by 35.
    The answer should be

    A. 71   B. 79   C. 87   D. 93

23. From $18.55 subtract $6.80.
    The answer should be

    A. $9.75   B. $10.95   C. $11.75   D. $25.35

3 (#1)

24. The sum of 2.75 + 4.50 + 3.60 is   24._____
    A. 9.75   B. 10.85   C. 11.15   D. 11.95

25. The sum of 9.63 + 11.21 + 17.25 is   25._____
    A. 36.09   B. 38.09   C. 39.92   D. 41.22

26. The sum of 112.0 + 16.9 + 3.84 is   26._____
    A. 129.3   B. 132.74   C. 136.48   D. 167.3

27. When 65 is added to the result of 14 multiplied by 13, the answer is   27._____
    A. 92   B. 182   C. 247   D. 16055

28. From $391.55 subtract $273.45.   28._____
    The answer should be
    A. $118.10   B. $128.20   C. $178.10   D. $218.20

29. When 119 is subtracted from the sum of 2016 + 1634, the answer is   29._____
    A. 2460   B. 3531   C. 3650   D. 3769

30. What is $367.20 + $510.00 + $402.80?   30._____
    A. $1,276.90   B. $1,277.90   C. $1,279.00   D. $1,280.00

31. Multiply 35 x 65 x 15.   31._____
    The answer should be
    A. 2275   B. 24265   C. 31145   D. 34125

32. Multiply 40 x 65 x 10.   32._____
    The answer should be
    A. 26000   B. 28000   C. 25200   D. 22300

33. The total amount of money represented by 43 half-dollars, 26 quarters, and 71 dimes is 33._____
    A. $28.00   B. $35.10   C. $44.30   D. $56.60

34. The total amount of money represented by 132 quarters, 97 dimes, and 220 nickels is   34._____
    A. $43.70   B. $44.20   C. $52.90   D. $53.70

35. The total amount of money represented by 40 quarters, 40 dimes, and 20 nickels is   35._____
    A. $14.50   B. $15.00   C. $15.50   D. $16.00

36. The sum of $29.61 + $101.53 + $943.64 is   36._____
    A. $983.88   B. $1074.78   C. $1174.98   D. $1341.42

37. The sum of $132.25 + $85.63 + $7056.44 is   37._____
    A. $1694.19   B. $7274.32   C. $8464.57   D. $9346.22

4 (#1)

38. The sum of 4010 + 1271 + 23 + 838 is   38.____

   A. 6142   B. 6162   C. 6242   D. 6362

39. What is the value of 3 twenty dollar bills, 5 ten dollar bills, 13 five dollar bills, and 43 one   39.____
   dollar bills?

   A. $218.00   B. $219.00   C. $220.00   D. $221.00

40. What is the value of 8 twenty dollar bills, 13 ten dollar bills, 27 five dollar bills, 3 two dollar   40.____
   bills, and 43 one dollar bills?

   A. $364.00   B. $374.00   C. $474.00   D. $485.00

41. What is the value of 6 twenty dollar bills, 8 ten dollar bills, 19 five dollar bills, and 37 one   41.____
   dollar bills?

   A. $232.00   B. $233.00   C. $332.00   D. $333.00

42. What is the value of 13 twenty dollar bills, 17 ten dollar bills, 24 five dollar bills, 7 two dol-   42.____
   lar bills, and 55 one dollar bills?

   A. $594.00   B. $599.00   C. $609.00   D. $619.00

43. What is the value of 7 half dollars, 9 quarters, 23 dimes, and 17 nickels?   43.____

   A. $7.80   B. $7.90   C. $8.80   D. $8.90

44. What is the value of 3 one dollar coins, 3 half dollars, 7 quarters, 13 dimes, and 27 nick-   44.____
   els?

   A. $7.80   B. $8.70   C. $8.80   D. $8.90

45. What is the value of 73 quarters?   45.____

   A. $18.25   B. $18.50   C. $18.75   D. $19.00

46. What is the value of 173 nickels?   46.____

   A. $8.55   B. $8.65   C. $8.75   D. $8.85

47. In checking a book of consecutively numbered Senior Citizen tickets, you find there are   47.____
   no tickets between number 13,383 and 13,833.
   How many tickets are missing?

   A. 448   B. 449   C. 450   D. 451

48. A ticket clerk begins her shift with 2,322 tickets. How many tickets will she have at the   48.____
   end of her shift if she sells 1,315 and collects 1,704 from the turnstiles during her shift?

   A. 2,687   B. 2,693   C. 2,711   D. 2,722

49. A ticket clerk has three books of tickets. One contains 273 tickets, one contains 342 tick-   49.____
   ets, and one contains 159 tickets. The clerk combines the contents of the three books
   and then sells 217 tickets.
   How many tickets are left?

   A. 556   B. 557   C. 568   D. 991

50. A ticket clerk has a quantity of consecutively numbered tickets. The number on the ticket having the lowest number is 27,069. The number on the ticket having the highest number is 27,154.
How many tickets does the clerk have?   50._____

   A. 84   B. 85   C. 86   D. 87

KEY (CORRECT ANSWERS)

1. D	11. C	21. D	31. D	41. C
2. C	12. C	22. B	32. A	42. D
3. B	13. A	23. C	33. B	43. D
4. C	14. D	24. B	34. D	44. D
5. C	15. A	25. B	35. B	45. A
6. A	16. C	26. B	36. B	46. B
7. B	17. B	27. C	37. B	47. B
8. A	18. A	28. A	38. A	48. C
9. A	19. D	29. B	39. A	49. B
10. D	20. C	30. D	40. C	50. C

6 (#1)

SOLUTIONS TO PROBLEMS

1. 53,632 + 27,403 + 98,765 + 75,424 = 255,224

2. 76,342 + 49,050 + 21,206 + 59,989 = 206,587

3. $452.13 + $963.83 + $621.25 = $2037.21

4. 36,392 + 42,156 + 98,765 = 177,313

5. 40,125 + 87,123 + 24,689 = 151,937

6. 2379 + 4015 + 6521 + 9986 = 22901

7. 50,962 - 36,197 = 14,765

8. 90,000 - 31,928 = 58,072

9. 63,764 - 21,548 = 42,216

10. $9605.13 - $2715.96 = $6889.17

11. 76,421 - 73,101 = 3320

12. $8.25 - $6.50 = $1.75

13. (563)(.50) = 281.50

14. (.35)(1045) = 365.75

15. (25)(2513) = 62,825

16. (423)(.01) = 4.23

17. (6.70)(3.2) = 21.44

18. (630)(517) = 325,710

19. (35)(846) = 29,610

20. (823)(.05) = 41.15

21. (1690)(.10) = 169

22. 2765 / 35 = 79

23. $18.55 - $6.80 = $11.75

24. 2.75 + 4.50 + 3.60 = 10.85

25. 9.63 + 11.21 + 17.25 = 38.09

26. 112.0 + 16.9 + 3.84 = 132.74

27. 65 + (14)(13) = 247

7 (#1)

28. $391.55 - $273.45 = $118.10

29. 2016 + 1634 - 119 = 3531

30. $367.20 + $510.00 + $402.80 = $1280.00

31. (35)(65)(15) = 34,125

32. (40)(65)(10) - 26,000

33. (43)(.50) + (26)(.25) + (71)(.10) = $35.10

34. (132)(.25) + (97)(.10) + (220)(.05) = $53.70

35. (40)(.25) + (40)(.10) + (20)(.05) = $15.00

36. $29.61 + $101.53 + $943.64 = $1074.78

37. $132.25 + $85.63 + $7056.44 = $7274.32

38. 4010 + 1271 + 23 + 838 = 6142

39. (3)($20) + (5)($10) + (13)($5) + (43)($1) + $218.00

40. (8)($20) + (13)($10) + (27)($5) + (3)($2) + (43)($1) = $474.00

41. (6)($20) + (8)($10) + (19)($5) + (37)($1) = $332.00

42. (13)($20) + (17)($10) + (24)($5) + (7)($2) + (55)($1) = $619.00

43. (7)(.50) + (9)(.25) + (23)(.10) + (17)(.05) = $8.90

44. (3)($1) + (3)(.50) + (7)(.25) + (13)(.10) + (27)(.05) = $8.90

45. (73)(.25) = $18.25

46. (173)(.05) = $8.65

47. The missing tickets are numbered 13,384 through 13,832.
    This represents 13,832 - 13,384 + 1 = 449 tickets.

48. 2322 - 1315 + 1704 = 2711 tickets left.

49. 273 + 342 + 159 - 217 = 557 tickets left

50. 27,154 - 27,069 + 1 = 86 tickets

ARITHMETICAL REASONING
EXAMINATION SECTION
TEST 1

DIRECTIONS: Each question or incomplete statement is followed by several suggested answers or completions. Select the one that BEST answers the question or completes the statement. *PRINT THE LETTER OF THE CORRECT ANSWER IN THE SPACE AT THE RIGHT.*

1. If a secretary answered 28 phone calls and typed the addresses for 112 credit statements in one morning, what is the RATIO of phone calls answered to credit statements typed for that period of time?

    A. 1:4 B. 1:7 C. 2:3 D. 3:5

    1.____

2. According to a suggested filing system, no more than 10 folders should be filed behind any one file guide and from 15 to 25 file guides should be used in each file drawer for easy finding and filing.
The MAXIMUM number of folders that a five-drawer file cabinet can hold to allow easy finding and filing is

    A. 550 B. 750 C. 1,100 D. 1,250

    2.____

3. An employee had a starting salary of $19,353. He received a salary increase at the end of each year, and at the end of the seventh year his salary was $25,107.
What was his AVERAGE annual increase in salary over these seven years?

    A. $765 B. $807 C. $822 D. $858

    3.____

4. The 55 typists and 28 senior clerks in a certain agency were paid a total of $1,457,400 in salaries in 2005.
If the average annual salary of a typist was $16,800, the average annual salary of a senior clerk was

    A. $19,050 B. $19,950 C. $20,100 D. $20,250

    4.____

5. A typist has been given a three-page report to type. She has finished typing the first two pages. The first page has 283 words, and the second page has 366 words.
If the total report consists of 954 words, how many words will she have to type on the third page of the report?

    A. 202 B. 287 C. 305 D. 313

    5.____

6. In one day, Clerk A processed 30% more forms than Clerk B, and Clerk C processed 1 1/4 as many forms as Clerk A.
If Clerk B processed 40 forms, how many more forms were processed by Clerk C than Clerk B?

    A. 12 B. 13 C. 21 D. 25

    6.____

7. A clerk who earns a gross salary of $678 every 2 weeks has the following deductions taken from her paycheck: 15% for city, state, and federal taxes; 2 1/2% for Social Security; $1.95 for health insurance; and $9.00 for union dues.
The amount of her take-home pay is

   A. $429.60   B. $468.60   C. $497.40   D. $548.40

8. In 2002, an agency spent $400 to buy pencils at a cost of $1.00 a dozen.
If the agency used 3/4 of these pencils in 2002 and used the same number of pencils in 2003, how many more pencils did it have to buy to have enough pencils for all of 2003?

   A. 1,200   B. 2,400   C. 3,600   D. 4,800

9. A clerk who worked in Agency X earned the following salaries: $15,105 the first year, $15,750 the second year, and $16,440 the third year. Another clerk who worked in Agency Y for three years earned $15,825 a year for two years and $16,086 the third year. The DIFFERENCE between the average salaries received by both clerks over a three-year period is

   A. $147   B. $153   C. $261   D. $423

10. An employee who works more than 40 hours in any week receives overtime payment for the extra hours at time and one-half (1 1/2 times) his hourly rate of pay. An employee who earns $13.60 an hour works a total of 45 hours during a certain week.
His TOTAL pay for that week would be

    A. $564.40   B. $612.00   C. $646.00   D. $824.00

11. Suppose that the amount of money spent for supplies in 2006 for a division in a city department was $156,500. This represented an increase of 12% over the amount spent for supplies for this division in 2005.
The amount of money spent for supplies for this division in 2005 was MOST NEARLY

    A. $139,730   B. $137,720   C. $143,460   D. $138,720

12. Suppose that a group of five clerks have been assigned to insert 24,000 letters into envelopes. The clerks perform this work at the following rates of speed: Clerk A, 1,100 letters an hour; Clerk B, 1,450 letters an hour; Clerk C, 1,200 letters an hour; Clerk D, 1,300 letters an hour; Clerk E, 1,250 letters an hour. At the end of two hours of work, Clerks C and D are assigned to another task.
From the time that Clerks C and D were taken off the assignment, the number of hours required for the remaining clerks to complete this assignment is

    A. less than 3 hours
    B. 3 hours
    C. more than 3 hours, but less than 4 hours
    D. more than 4 hours

13. The number 60 is 40% of

    A. 24   B. 84   C. 96   D. 150

14. If 3/8 of a number is 96, the number is

    A. 132   B. 36   C. 256   D. 156

15. A city department uses an average of 25 20-cent, 35 30-cent, and 350 40-cent postage stamps each day.
    The TOTAL cost of stamps used by the department in a five-day period is

    A. $29.50   B. $155.50   C. $290.50   D. $777.50

    15._____

16. A city department issued 12,000 applications in 2000. The number of applications that the department issued in 1998 was 25% greater than the number it issued in 2000.
    If the department issued 10% fewer applications in 1996 than it did in 1998, the number it issued in 1996 was

    A. 16,500   B. 13,500   C. 9,900   D. 8,100

    16._____

17. A clerk can add 40 columns of figures an hour by using an adding machine and 20 columns of figures an hour without using an adding machine.
    The TOTAL number of hours it would take him to add 200 columns if he does 3/5 of the work by machine and the rest without the machine is

    A. 6   B. 7   C. 8   D. 9

    17._____

18. In 1997, a city department bought 500 dozen pencils at $1.20 per dozen. In 2000, only 75 percent as many pencils were bought as were bought in 1997, but the price was 20 percent higher than the 1997 price. The TOTAL cost of the pencils bought in 2000 was

    A. $540   B. $562.50   C. $720   D. $750

    18._____

19. A clerk is assigned to check the accuracy of the entries on 490 forms. He checks 40 forms an hour. After working one hour on this task, he is joined by another clerk, who checks these forms at the rate of 35 an hour.
    The TOTAL number of hours required to do the entire assignment is

    A. 5   B. 6   C. 7   D. 8

    19._____

20. Assume that there are a total of 420 employees in a city agency. Thirty percent of the employees are clerks, and 1/7 are typists.
    The DIFFERENCE between the number of clerks and the number of typists is

    A. 126   B. 66   C. 186   D. 80

    20._____

21. Assume that a duplicating machine produces copies of a bulletin at a cost of 2 cents per copy. The machine produces 120 copies of the bulletin per minute.
    If the cost of producing a certain number of copies was $12, how many minutes of operation did it take the machine to produce this number of copies?

    A. 5   B. 2   C. 10   D. 6

    21._____

22. An assignment is completed by 32 clerks in 22 days. Assuming that all the clerks work at the same rate of speed, the number of clerks that would be needed to complete this assignment in 16 days is

    A. 27   B. 38   C. 44   D. 52

    22._____

23. A department head hired a total of 60 temporary employees to handle a seasonal increase in the department's workload. The following lists the number of temporary employees hired, their rates of pay, and the duration of their employment:

    One-third of the total were hired as clerks, each at the rate of $27,500 a year, for two months.

    30 percent of the total were hired as office machine operators, each at the rate of $31,500 a year, for four months.

    22 stenographers were hired, each at the rate of $30,000 a year, for three months.

The total amount paid to these temporary employees was MOST NEARLY

  A. $1,780,000   B. $450,000
  C. $650,000   D. $390,000

24. Assume that there are 2,300 employees in a city agency. Also, assume that five percent of these employees are accountants, that 80 percent of the accountants have college degrees, and that one-half of the accountants who have college degrees have five years of experience. Then, the number of employees in the agency who are accountants with college degrees and five years of experience is

  A. 46   B. 51   C. 460   D. 920

25. Assume that the regular 8-hour working day of a laborer is from 8 A.M. to 5 P.M., with an hour off for lunch. He earns a regular hourly rate of pay for these 8 hours and is paid at the rate of time-and-a-half for each hour worked after his regular working day.

If, on a certain day, he works from 8 A.M. to 6 P.M., with an hour off for lunch, and earns $171, his regular hourly rate of pay is

  A. $16.30   B. $17.10   C. $18.00   D. $19.00

KEY (CORRECT ANSWERS)

1. A		11. A	
2. D		12. B	
3. C		13. D	
4. A		14. C	
5. C		15. D	
6. D		16. B	
7. D		17. B	
8. B		18. A	
9. A		19. C	
10. C		20. B	

21. A
22. C
23. B
24. A
25. C

SOLUTIONS TO PROBLEMS

1. 28/112 is equivalent to 1:4

2. Maximum number of folders = (10)(25)(5) = 1250

3. Average annual increase = ($25,107-19,353) ÷ 7 = $822

4. $1,457,400 - (55)($16,800) = $533,400 = total amount paid to senior clerks. Average senior clerk's salary = $533,400 ÷ 28 = $19,050

5. Number of words on 3rd page = 954 - 283 - 366 = 305

6. Clerk A processed (40)(1.30) = 52 forms and clerk C processed (52)(1.25) = 65 forms. Finally, 65 - 40 = 25

7. Take-home pay = $678 - (.15)($678) - (.025)($678) - $1.95 - $9.00 = $548.40

8. (400)(12) = 4800 pencils. In 2002, (3/4)(4800) = 3600 were used, so that 1200 pencils were available at the beginning of 2003. Since 3600 pencils were also used in 2003, the agency had to buy 3600 - 1200 = 2400 pencils.

9. Average salary for clerk in Agency X = ($15,105+$15,750+$16,440)/3 = $15,765. Average salary for clerk in Agency Y = ($15,825+ $15,825+$16,086) ÷ 3 = $15,912. Difference in average salaries = $147.

10. Total pay = ($13.60)(40) + ($20.40)(5) = $646.00

11. In 2005, amount spent = $156,500 ÷ 1.12 ≈ $139,730 (Actual value = $139,732.1429)

12. At the end of 2 hours, (1100)(2) + (1450)(2) + (1200)(2) + (1300X2) + (1250X2) = 12,600 letters have been inserted into envelopes. The remaining 11,400 letters done by clerks A, B, and C will require 11,400 ÷ (1100+1450+1250) = 3 hours.

13. 60 ÷ .40 = 150

14. 96 ÷ 3/8 = (96)(8/3) = 256

15. Total cost = (5)[(25)(.20)+(35)(.30)+(350)(.40)]= $777.50

16. In 1998, (12,000) (1.25) = 15,000 applications were issued In 1996, (15,000)(.90) = 13,500 applications were issued

17. Total number of hours $=\dfrac{120}{40} + \dfrac{80}{20} = 7$

18. (.75)(500 dozen) = 375 dozen purchased in 2000 at a cost of ($1.20)(1.20) = $1.44 per dozen. Total cost for 2000 = ($1.44) (375) = $540

19. Total time = 1 hour + 450/75 hrs. = 7 hours

20. (.30)(420) - (1/7)(420) = 126 - 60 = 66

21. Cost per minute = (120)(.02) = $2.40. Then, $12 ÷ $2.40 = 5 minutes

22. (32)(22) ÷ 16 = 44 clerks

23. Total amount paid = (20)($27,500)(2/12) + (18)($31,500)(4/12) + (22)($30,000)(3/12) = $445,666.$\overline{6}$ ≈ $450,000

24. Number of accountants with college degrees and five years of experience = (2300)(.05)(.80)(1/2) = 46

25. Let x = regular hourly pay. Then, (8)(x) + (1)(1.5x) = $1.71 So, 9.5x = 171. Solving, x = $18

TEST 2

DIRECTIONS: Each question or incomplete statement is followed by several suggested answers or completions. Select the one that BEST answers the question or completes the statement. *PRINT THE LETTER OF THE CORRECT ANSWER IN THE SPACE AT THE RIGHT.*

1. Assume that you know the capacity of a filing cabinet, the extent of which it is filled, and the daily rate at which material is being added to the file.
   In order to estimate how many more days it will take for the cabinet to be filled to capacity, you should

   A. divide the extent to which the cabinet is filled by the daily rate
   B. take the difference between the capacity of the cabinet and the material in it, and multiply the result by the daily rate of adding material
   C. divide the daily rate of adding material by the difference between the capacity of the cabinet and the material in it
   D. take the difference between the capacity of the cabinet and the material in it, and divide the result by the daily rate of adding material

   1._____

2. Suppose you have been asked to compute the average salary earned in your department during the past year. For each of the divisions of the department, you are given the number of employees and the average salary.
   In order to find the requested overall average salary for the department, you should

   A. add the average salaries of the various divisions and divide the total by the number of divisions
   B. multiply the number of employees in each division by the corresponding average salary, add the results and divide the total by the number of employees in the department
   C. add the average salaries of the various divisions and divide the total by the total number of employees in the department
   D. multiply the sum of the average salaries of the various divisions by the total number of divisions and divide the resulting product by the total number of employees in the department

   2._____

3. Suppose that a group of six clerks has been assigned to assemble the duplicated pages of a report into completed copies. After four hours of work, they have been able to complete one-third of the job.
   In order to assemble all the remaining copies in three more hours of work, the number of clerks which will have to be added to the original six, assuming that all the clerks assigned to this task work at the same rate of speed, is

   A. 10   B. 16   C. 2   D. 6

   3._____

4. A study of the grades of students in a certain college revealed that in 2005, 15% fewer students received a passing grade in mathematics than in 2004, whereas in 2006 the number of students passing mathematics increased 15% over 2005.
   On the basis of this study, it would be MOST accurate to conclude that

   A. the same percentage of students passed mathematics in 2004 as in 2006
   B. of the three years studied, the greatest percentage of students passed mathematics in 2006

   4._____

89

C. the percentage of students who passed mathematics in 2006 was less than the percentage passing this subject in 2004
D. the percentage of students passing mathematics in 2004 was 15% greater than the percentage of students passing this subject in 2006

5. A city department employs 1,400 people, of whom 35% are clerks and 1/8 are stenographers.
   The number of employees in the department who are neither clerks nor stenographers is

   A. 640   B. 665   C. 735   D. 760

6. Assume that there are 190 papers to be filed and that Clerk A and Clerk B are assigned to file these papers. If Clerk A files 40 papers more than Clerk B, then the number of papers that Clerk A files is

   A. 75   B. 110   C. 115   D. 150

7. A stock clerk had on hand the following items:
   500 pads, each worth 16 cents
   130 pencils, each worth 12 cents
   50 dozen rubber bands, worth 8 cents a dozen
   If, from this stock, he issued 125 pads, 45 pencils, and 48 rubber bands, the value of the remaining stock would be

   A. $25.72   B. $27.80   C. $70.52   D. $73.88

8. In a particular agency, there were 160 accidents in 2002. Of these accidents, 75% were due to unsafe acts and the rest were due to unsafe conditions. In the following year, a special safety program was established. The number of accidents in 2004 due to unsafe acts was reduced to 35% of what it had been in 2002.
   How many accidents due to unsafe acts were there in 2004?

   A. 20   B. 36   C. 42   D. 56

9. At the end of every month, the petty cash fund of Agency A is reimbursed for payments made from the fund during the month. During the month of February, the amounts paid from the fund were entered on receipts as follows: 10 bus fares of $1.40 each and one taxi fare of $14.00. At the end of the month, the money left in the fund was in the following denominations: 60 one-dollar bills, 16 quarters, 40 dimes, and 80 nickels.
   If the petty cash fund is reduced by 20% for the following month, how much money will there be available in the petty cash fund for March?

   A. $44   B. $80   C. $86   D. $100

10. An employee worked on a job for 6 weeks, 5 days per week, and 8 hours per day. How many hours did he work on the job?

    A. 40   B. 48   C. 55   D. 240

11. Divide 35 by .7.

    A. 5   B. 42   C. 50   D. 245

12. .1% of 25 =

    A. .025   B. .25   C. 2.5   D. 25

13. In a city agency, 80 percent of the total number of employees are more than 25 years of age and 65 percent of the total number of employees are high school graduates.
    The SMALLEST possible percent of employees who are both high school graduates and more than 25 years of age is

    A. 35%   B. 45%   C. 55%   D. 65%

14. Two clerical units, X and Y, each having a different number of clerks, are assigned to file registration cards. It takes Unit X, which contains 8 clerks, 21 days to file the same number of cards that Unit Y can file in 28 days. It is also a fact that Unit X can file 174,528 cards in 72 days.
    Assuming that all the clerks in both units work at the same rate of speed, the number of cards which can be filed by Unit Y in 144 days, if 4 more clerks are added to the staff of Unit Y, is MOST NEARLY

    A. 392,000   B. 436,000   C. 523,000   D. 669,000

15. Assume that two machines, each costing $14,750, were purchased for your office. Each machine requires the services of an operator at a salary of $2,000 per month. These machines are to replace six clerks, two of whom earn $1,550 per month each, and four of whom earn $1,700 per month each.
    The number of months it will take for the cost of the machines to be made up from the savings in salaries is

    A. less than four   B. four
    C. five   D. more than five

16. Suppose that the amount of stationery used by your department in August decreased by 16% as compared with the amount used in July, and that the amount used in September increased by 25% as compared with the amount used in August.
    The amount of stationery used in September as compared with the amount used in July is

    A. greater by 5 percent   B. less by 5 percent
    C. greater by 9 percent   D. the same

17. An employee earns $48 a day and works 5 days a week.
    He will earn $2,160 in _____ weeks.

    A. 5   B. 7   C. 8   D. 9

18. In a certain bureau, the entire staff consists of 1 senior supervisor, 2 supervisors, 6 assistant supervisors, and 54 associate workers.
    The percent of the staff who are not associate workers is MOST NEARLY

    A. 14   B. 21   C. 27   D. 32

19. In a certain bureau, five employees each earn $1,000 a month, another 3 employees each earn $2,200 a month, and another two employees each earn $1,400 a month.
    The monthly payroll for these employees is

    A. $3,600   B. $8,800   C. $11,400   D. $14,400

20. An employee contributes 5% of his salary to the pension fund. 20.____
    If his salary is $1,200 a month, the amount of his contribution to the pension fund in a year is

    A. $480   B. $720   C. $960   D. $1,200

21. The number of square feet in an area that is 50 feet long and 30 feet wide is 21.____

    A. 80   B. 150   C. 800   D. 1,500

22. A farm hand was paid a weekly wage of $332.16 for a 48-hour work week. As a result of 22.____
    a new labor contract, he is paid $344.96 a week for a 44-hour work week with time and one-half pay for time worked in excess of 44 hours in any work week.
    If he continues to work 48 hours weekly under the new contract, the amount by which his average hourly rate for a 48-hour work week under the new contract exceeds the hourly rate previously paid him lies between _____ and _____ cents, inclusive.

    A. 91;100   B. 101;110   C. 111;120   D. 121;130

23. Each side of a square room, which is being used as an office, measures 66 feet. The 23.____
    floor of the room is divided by six traffic aisles, each aisle being six feet wide. Three of the aisles run parallel to the east and west sides of the room, and the other three run parallel to the north and south sides of the room, so that the remaining floor space is divided into 16 equal sections. If all of the floor space which is not being used for traffic aisles is occupied by desk and chair sets, and each set takes up 24 square feet of floor space, the number of desk and chair sets in the room is

    A. 80   B. 64   C. 36   D. 96

24. In 2005, a city agency bought 12,000 envelopes at $4.00 per hundred. In 2006, the price 24.____
    of envelopes purchased was 40 percent higher than the 2005 price, but only 60 percent as many envelopes were bought.
    The total cost of the envelopes purchased in 2006 was MOST NEARLY

    A. $250   B. $320   C. $400   D. $480

25. In a city agency, 25 percent of the women employees and 50 percent of the men employ- 25.____
    ees attended a general staff meeting.
    If 48 percent of all the employees in the agency are women, the percentage of all the employees who attended the meeting is

    A. 36%   B. 37%   C. 38%   D. 75%

KEY (CORRECT ANSWERS)

1. D
2. B
3. A
4. C
5. C

6. C
7. D
8. C
9. B
10. D

11. C
12. A
13. B
14. A
15. C

16. A
17. D
18. A
19. D
20. B

21. D
22. D
23. D
24. C
25. C

SOLUTIONS TO PROBLEMS

1. To determine number of days required to fill cabinet to capacity, subtract material in it from capacity amount, then divide by daily rate of adding material. Example: A cabinet already has 10 folders in it, and the capacity is 100 folders. Suppose 5 folders per day are added. Number of days to fill to capacity = (100-10) ÷ 5 = 18

2. To determine overall average salary, multiply number of employees in each division by that division's average salary, add results, then divide by total number of employees. Example: Division A has 4 employees with average salary of $40,000; division B has 6 employees with average salary of $36,000; division C has 2 employees with average salary of $46,000. Average salary = [(4)($40,000)+(6)($36,000)+(2)($46,000)] / 12 = $39,000

3. (6)(4) = 24 clerk-hours. Since only one-third of work has been done, (24) (3) - 24 = 48 clerk-hours remain. Then, 48 3 = 16 clerks. Thus, 16 - 6 = 10 additional clerks.

4. The percentage of students passing math in 2006 was less than the percentage of those passing math in 2004. Example: Suppose 400 students passed math in 2004. Then, (400)(.85) = 340 passed in 2005. Finally, (340)(1.15) = 391 passed in 2006.

5. 1400 - (.35)(1400) - (1/8)(1400) = 735

6. Let x = number of papers filed by clerk A, x-40 = number of papers filed by clerk B. Then, x + (x-40) = 190 Solving, x = 115

7. (500-125)(.16) + (130-45)(.12) + (50 - 48/12)(.08) = $60.00 + $10.20 + $3.68 = $73.88

8. (160)(.75) = 120 accidents due to unsafe acts in 2002. In 2004, (120)(.35) = 42 accidents due to unsafe acts

9. Original amount at beginning of February in the fund = (10)($1.40) + (1)($14.00) + (60)($1) + (16)(.25) + (40)(.10) + (80)(.05) = $100. Finally, for March, ($100)(.80) = $80 will be available

10. Total hours = (6)(5)(8) = 240

11. 35 ÷ .7 = 50

12. .1% of 25 = (.001)(25) = .025

13. Let A = percent of employees who are at least 25 years old and B = percent of employees who are high school graduates. Also, let N = percent of employees who fit neither category and J = percent of employees who are in both categories. Then, 100 = A + B + N - J. Substituting, 100 = 80 + 65 + N - J To minimize J, let N = 0. So, 100 = 80 + 65 + 0 - J. Solving, J = 45

14. Let Y = number of clerks in Unit Y. Then, (8)(21) = (4)(28), so Y = 6. Unit X has 8 clerks who can file 174,528 cards in 72 flays; thus, each clerk in Unit X can file 174,528 ÷ 72 ÷ 8 = 303 cards per day. Adding 4 clerks to Unit Y will yield 10 clerks in that unit. Since their rate is equal to that of Unit X, the clerks in Unit Y will file, in 144 days, is (303)(10)(144) = 436,320 ≈ 436,000 cards.

15. Let x = required number of months. The cost of the machines in x months = (2)(14,750) + (2)(2000)(x) = 29,500 + 4000x. The savings in salaries for the displaced clerks = x[(2)(1550) +(4)(1700)] = 9900x. Thus, 29,500 + 4000x = 9900x. Solving, x = 5. So, five months will elapse in order to achieve a savings in cost.

16. Let x = amount used in July, so that .84x = amount used in August. For September, the amount used = (.84x)(1.25) = 1.05x. This means the amount used in September is 5% more than the amount used in July.

17. Each week he earns ($48)(5) = $240. Then, $2160 ÷ $240 = 9 weeks

18. (1+2+6) ÷ 63 = 1/7 ≈ 14%

19. Monthly payroll = (5)($1000) + (3)($2200) + (2)($1400) = $14,400

20. Yearly contribution to pension fund = (12)($1200)(.05) = $720

21. (50')(30') = 1500 sq.ft.

22. Old rate = 332.16 ÷ 48 = 6.92 (48 hours)
    New rate = 344.96 (44 hours)
    Overtime rate = 344.96 ÷ 44 = 7.75/hr. x 1.5 x 4 = 46.48
    344.96 + 46.48 = 391.44
    391.44 ÷ 48 = 8.15
    815 - 692 = 123 cents an hour more

23. Each of the 16 sections is a square with side [66'-(3)(6')] ÷ 4 = 12'. So each section contains (12')(12') = 144 sq.ft.
    The number of desk and chair sets = (144 ÷ 24) (16) = 96

24. In 2006, (.60)(12,000) = 7200 envelopes were bought and the price per hundred was ($4.00)(1.40) = $5.60. The total cost = (5.60)(72) = $403.20 ≈ $400

25. (.25)(.48) + (.50)(.52) = .38 = 38%

TEST 3

DIRECTIONS: Each question or incomplete statement is followed by several suggested answers or completions. Select the one that BEST answers the question or completes the statement. *PRINT THE LETTER OF THE CORRECT ANSWER IN THE SPACE AT THE RIGHT.*

1. According to one suggested filing system, no more than 12 folders should be filed behind any one file guide and from 10 to 20 file guides should be used in each file drawer. Based on this filing system, the MAXIMUM number of folders that a four-drawer file cabinet can hold is

   A. 240 B. 480 C. 960 D. 1,200

   1._____

2. A certain office uses three different forms. Last year, it used 3,500 copies of Form L, 6,700 copies of Form M, and 10,500 copies of Form P. This year, the office expects to decrease the use of each of these forms by 5%. The TOTAL number of these three forms which the office expects to use this year is

   A. 10,350 B. 16,560 C. 19,665 D. 21,735

   2._____

3. The hourly rate of pay for a certain part-time employee is computed by dividing his yearly salary rate by the number of hours in the work year. The employee's yearly salary rate is $18,928, and there are 1,820 hours in the work year.
   If this employee works 18 hours during one week, his TOTAL earnings for these 18 hours are

   A. $180.00 B. $183.60 C. $187.20 D. $190.80

   3._____

4. Assume that the regular work week of an employee is 35 hours and that the employee is paid for any extra hours worked according to the following schedule. For hours worked in excess of 35 hours, up to and including 40 hours, the employee receives his regular hourly rate of pay. For hours worked in excess of 40 hours, the employee receives 1 1/2 times his hourly rate of pay.
   If the employee's hourly rate of pay is $11.20 and he works 43 hours during a certain week, his TOTAL pay for the week would be

   A. $481.60 B. $498.40 C. $556.00 D. $722.40

   4._____

5. A clerk divided his 35 hour work week as follows:
   1/5 of his time in sorting mail;
   1/2 of his time in filing letters; and
   1/7 of his time in reception work.
   The rest of his time was devoted to messenger work. The percentage of time spent on messenger work by the clerk during the week was MOST NEARLY

   A. 6% B. 10% C. 14% D. 16%

   5._____

6. A city department has set up a computing unit and has rented 5 computing machines at a yearly rental of $700 per machine. In addition, the cost to the department for the maintenance and repair of each of these machines is $50 per year. Five computing machine operators, each receiving an annual salary of $15,000, and a supervisor, who receives $19,000 a year, have been assigned to this unit. This unit will perform the work previously performed by 10 employees whose combined salary was $162,000 a year.
   On the basis of these facts, the savings that will result from the operation of this computing unit for 5 years will be MOST NEARLY

   A. $250,000 B. $320,000 C. $330,000 D. $475,000

   6._____

7. Twelve clerks are assigned to enter certain data on index cards. This number of clerks could perform the task in 18 days. After these clerks have worked on this assignment for 6 days, 4 more clerks are added to the staff to do this work.
Assuming that all the clerks work at the same rate of speed, the entire task, instead of taking 18 days, will be performed in _____ days.

   A. 9 B. 12 C. 15 D. 16

8. Suppose that a file cabinet, which has a capacity of 3,000 cards, now contains approximately 2,200 cards. Cards are added to the file at the average rate of 30 cards a day.
To find the number of days it will take to fill the cabinet to capacity,

   A. divide 3,000 by 30
   B. divide 2,200 by 3,000
   C. divide 800 by 30
   D. multiply 30 by the fraction 2,200 divided by 3,000

9. Six gross of special drawing pencils were purchased for use in a city department. If the pencils were used at the rate of 24 a week, the MAXIMUM number of weeks that the six gross of pencils would last is _____ weeks.

   A. 6 B. 12 C. 24 D. 36

10. A stock clerk had 600 pads on hand. He then issued 3/8 of his supply of pads to Division X, 1/4 to Division Y, and 1/6 to Division Z.
The number of pads remaining in stock is

    A. 48 B. 125 C. 240 D. 475

11. If a certain job can be performed by 18 clerks in 26 days, the number of clerks needed to perform the job in 12 days is _____ clerks.

    A. 24 B. 30 C. 39 D. 52

12. In anticipation of a seasonal increase in the amount of work to be performed by his division, a division chief prepared the following list of additional temporary employees needed by his division and the amount of time they would be employed:
    26 cashiers, each at $24,000 a year, for 2 months
    15 laborers, each at $85.00 a day, for 50 days
    6 clerks, each at $21,000 a year, for 3 months
The total approximate cost for this additional personnel would be MOST NEARLY

    A. $200,000 B. $250,000 C. $500,000 D. $600,000

13. A copy machine company offered to sell a city agency 4 copy machines at a discount of 15% from the list price, and to allow the agency $850 for each of its two old machines. The list price of the new machines is $6,250 per machine.
If the city agency accepts this offer, the amount of money it will have to provide for the purchase of these 4 machines is

    A. $17,350 B. $22,950 C. $19,550 D. $18,360

14. A stationery buyer was offered bond paper at the following price scale:
    $1.43 per ream for the first 1,000 reams
    $1.30 per ream for the next 4,000 reams
    $1.20 per ream for each additional ream beyond 5,000 reams
    If the buyer ordered 10,000 reams of paper, the average cost per ream, computed to the nearest cent, was

    A. $1.24   B. $1.26   C. $1.31   D. $1.36

15. A clerk has 5.70 percent of his salary deducted for his retirement pension. If this clerk's annual salary is $20,400, the monthly deduction for his retirement pension is

    A. $298.20   B. $357.90   C. $1,162.80   D. $96.90

16. In a certain bureau, two-thirds of the employees are clerks and the remainder are typists. If there are 90 clerks, then the number of typists in this bureau is

    A. 135   B. 45   C. 120   D. 30

17. The number of investigations conducted by an agency in 1999 was 3,600. In 2000, the number of investigations conducted was one-third more than in 1999. The number of investigations conducted in 2001 was three-fourths of the number conducted in 2000. It is anticipated that the number of investigations conducted in 2002 will be equal to the average of the three preceding years. On the basis of this information, the MOST accurate of the following statements is that the number of investigations conducted in

    A. 1999 is larger than the number anticipated for 2002
    B. 2000 is smaller than the number anticipated for 2002
    C. 2001 is equal to the number conducted in 1999
    D. 2001 is larger than the number anticipated in 2002

18. A city agency engaged in repair work uses a small part which the city purchases for 14¢ each. Assume that, in a certain year, the total expenditure of the city for this part was $700.
    How many of these parts were purchased that year?

    A. 50   B. 200   C. 2,000   D. 5,000

19. The work unit which you supervise is responsible for processing 15 reports per month. If your unit has 4 clerks and the best worker completes 40% of the reports himself, how many reports would each of the other clerks have to complete if they all do an equal number?

    A. 1   B. 2   C. 3   D. 4

20. Assume that the work unit in which you work has 24 clerks and 18 stenographers. In order to change the ratio of stenographers to clerks so that there is 1 stenographer for every 4 clerks, it would be necessary to REDUCE the number of stenographers by

   A. 3   B. 6   C. 9   D. 12

21. The arithmetic mean salary for five employees earning $18,500, $18,300, $18,600, $18,400, and $18,500, respectively, is

   A. $18,450   B. $18,460   C. $18,475   D. $18,500

22. Last year, a city department which is responsible for purchasing supplies ordered bond paper in equal quantities from 22 different companies. The price was exactly the same for each company, and the total cost for the 22 orders was $693,113.
Assuming prices did not change during the year, the cost of each order was MOST NEARLY

   A. $31,490   B. $31,495   C. $31,500   D. $31,505

23. Suppose that a large bureau has 187 employees. On a particular day, approximately 14% of these employees are not available for work because of absences due to vacation, illness, or other reasons. Of the remaining employees, 1/7 are assigned to a special project while the balance are assigned to the normal work of the bureau. The number of employees assigned to the normal work of the bureau on that day is

   A. 112   B. 124   C. 138   D. 142

24. Suppose that you are in charge of a typing pool of 8 typists. Two typists type at the rate of 38 words per minute; three type at the rate of 40 words per minute; three type at the rate of 42 words per minute. The average typewritten page consists of 50 lines, 12 words per line. Each employee works from 9 to 5 with one hour off for lunch.
The total number of pages typed by this pool in one day is, on the average, CLOSEST to _____ pages.

   A. 205   B. 225   C. 250   D. 275

25. Suppose that part-time workers are paid $7.20 an hour, prorated to the nearest half hour, with pay guaranteed for a minimum of four hours if services are required for less than four hours. In one operation, part-time workers signed the time sheet as follows:

Worker	In	Out
A	8:00 A.M.	11:35 A.M.
B	8:30 A.M.	3:20 P.M.
C	7:55 A.M.	11:00 A.M.
D	8:30 A.M.	2:25 P.M.

   How much would TOTAL payment to these part-time workers amount to for this operation, assuming that those who stayed after 12 Noon were not paid for one hour which they took off for lunch?

   A. $134.40   B. $136.80   C. $142.20   D. $148.80

KEY (CORRECT ANSWERS)

1. C
2. C
3. C
4. B
5. D

6. B
7. C
8. C
9. D
10. B

11. C
12. A
13. C
14. B
15. D

16. B
17. C
18. D
19. C
20. D

21. B
22. D
23. C
24. B
25. B

SOLUTIONS TO PROBLEMS

1. Maximum number of folders = (4)(12)(20) = 960

2. (3500+6700+10,500)(.95) = 19,665

3. Hourly rate = $18,928 ÷ 1820 = $10.40. Then, the pay for 18 hours = ($10.40)(18) = $187.20

4. Total pay = ($11.20)(40) + ($11.20)(1.5)(3) = $498.40

5. (1 - 1/5 - 1/2 - 1/7)(100)% ≈ 16%

6. Previous cost for five years = ($324,000)(5) = $1,620,000
   Present cost for five years = (5)(5)($1,400) + (5)(5)($100) + (5)(5)($30,000) + (1)(5)($38,000) = $977,500   The net savings = $642,500 ≈ $640,000

7. (12)(18) = 216 clerk-days. Then, 216 - (12)(6) = 144 clerk-days of work left when 4 more clerks are added. Now, 16 clerks will finish the task in 144 ÷ 16 = 9 more days. Finally, the task will require a total of 6 + 9 = 15 days.

8. Number of days needed = (3000-2200) ÷ 30 = 26.7, which is equivalent to dividing 800 by 30.

9. (6)(144) = 864 pencils purchased. Then, 864 ÷ 24 = 36 maximum number of weeks

10. Number of remaining pads = 600 - (1)(600) - (1/4)(600) - (1/6)(600) = 125

11. (18)(26) ÷ 12 = 39 clerks

12. Total cost = (26)($24,000)(2/12) + (15)($85)(50) + (6)($21,000)(3/12) = $199,250 $200,000

13. (4)($6250)(.85) - (2)($850) = $19,550

14. Total cost = ($1.43)(1000) + ($1.30)(4000) + ($1.20X5000) = $12,630. Average cost per ream = $12,630 10,000 ≈ $1.26

15. Monthly salary = $20,400 ÷ 12 = $1700. Thus, the monthly deduction for his pension = ($1700)(.057) + $96.90

16. Number of employees = 90 ÷ 2/3 = 135. Then, the number of typists = (1/3)(135) = 45

17. The number of investigations for each year is as follows:
    1999: 3600
    2000: (3600)(1 1/3) = 4800
    2001: (4800)(3/4) = 3600
    2002: (3600+4800+3600)/3 = 4000
    So, the number of investigations were equal for 1999 and 2001.

18. $700 ÷ .14 = 5000 parts

19. The best worker does (.40)(15) = 6 reports. The other 9 reports are divided equally among the other 3 clerks, so each clerk does 9 ÷ 3 = 3 reports.

20. 1:4 = 6:24 . Thus, the number of stenographers must be reduced by 18 - 6 = 12

21. Mean = ($18,500+$18,300+$18,400+$18,500) ÷ 5 = $18,460

22. The cost per order = $693,113 ÷ 22 ≈ $31,505

23. 187 - (.14) = 26. 187 - 26 = 161 - 1/7 (161) = 23
    161 - 23 = 138

24. Number of words typed in 1 min. = (2)(38) + (3)(40) + (3)(42) = 322. For 7 hours, the total number of words typed = (7)(60)(322) = 135,240. Each page contains (on the average) (50)(12) = 600 words. Finally, 135,240 ÷ 600 ≈ 225 pages

25. Worker A = ($7.20)(4) = $28.80
    Worker B = ($7.20)(3 1/2) + ($7.20)(2 1/2) = $43.20
    Worker C = ($7.20)(4) = $28.80
    Worker D = ($7.20)(3 1/2) + ($7.20)(1 1/2) = $36.00
    Total for all 4 workers = $136.80
    Note: Workers A and C received the guaranteed minimum 4 hours pay each.

ARITHMETICAL REASONING

EXAMINATION SECTION

TEST 1

DIRECTIONS: Each question or incomplete statement is followed by several suggested answers or completions. Select the one that BEST answers the question or completes the statement. *PRINT THE LETTER OF THE CORRECT ANSWER IN THE SPACE AT THE RIGHT.*

1. The initial mark-up in a store is 40%; mark-downs are 5%; shortages 1%; cash discounts 5%; alteration costs 5%; expenses 25%.
   The maintained mark-up is
   A. 34%   B. 39%   C. 36.4%   D. 30%

   1.____

2. A buyer of TV sets wishes to maintain a mark-up of 37½% after all mark-downs are taken. Of 25 sets costing $150 each, he sells 20 at $265.
   How much can he mark-down the remaining 5 sets and still realize his mark-up objective?
   A. $166   B. $150   C. $140   D. $125

   2.____

3. An article originally selling for $12 and costing $8 was marked down to $10. Assuming the same mark-up, what is the present market value of its cost?
   A. $6.68   B. $8.00   C. $5.67   D. $6.86

   3.____

4. What is the *on* percentage of trade discounts of 20% and 10%?
   A. 70   B. 85   C. 72   D. 80

   4.____

5. Canadian cost of a sweater is $40. Packing and labor cost $5.00; ad valorem duty, 40%; specific duty, 65¢; rate of exchange, .9091.
   What is the duty in American currency?
   A. $16.96   B. $16.36   C. $18.00   D. $18.60

   5.____

6. A bolt of cloth measures 40 yards. The following yardages are sold: 4½, 5¾, 6⅞.
   How many yards are left?
   A. 23⅞   B. 22½   C. 22⅞   D. 24⅜

   6.____

7. A shirt manufacturer has 76½ yards of broadcloth to be used for shirts.
   If each shirt takes 2½ yards, how many shirts can he make?
   A. 38   B. 30   C. 19   D. 31

   7.____

8. Subtract 1.003 from 24.5.
   A. 24.003   B. 12.42   C. 23.2   D. 23.497

   8.____

9. A store carries a stock amounting to $265,830.25. Cash discounts, on the average, amount to 5¼%.
   How much are the cash discounts?
   A. $13,956.09   B. $1,395.61   C. $139.56   D. $1.39

   9.____

10. If the sales in a department totaled $67,507.50 and the average sale was $22.50, how many transactions were there?
    A. 3,000   B. 300   C. 30,000   D. 0

    10.____

11. A department store reports a decrease in sales of 5.5% for this year. If this year's sales are $275,825,000, last year's sales were
    A. $291,878,000   B. $290,995,000
    C. $260,655,000   D. $290,788,000

    11.____

12. For the current year, the sales volume in a store was $50,000,000. Other income amounted to $1,500,000, operating expenses were $10,000,000; cost of goods sold, $37,500,000.
    What is the percent of net profit based on retail?
    A. 10   B. 8   C. 50   D. 13

    12.____

13. If this year's sales shown an increase of 300% over last year, this year's sales are how many times last year's sales?
    A. 3   B. 1⅓   C. 4   D. ¼

    13.____

14. Net sales in a shop amounted to $374,000; returns were 10%; allowances 5%. What were the gross sales?
    A. $430,100   B. $415,000   C. $411,400   D. $440,000

    14.____

15. If the average sale in a store is expected to rise 5% over last year, and the number of transactions increases 3%, what percentage of increase in dollar sales volume should be planned?
    A. 8   B. 4   C. 8.15   D. 8.51

    15.____

16. The billed cost on an invoice is $300; freight charges, $10; cash discount, 2%; the retail value of the merchandise is $525.
    The mark-up percent on retail is
    A. 40.9   B. 42   C. 69   D. 69.5

    16.____

17. A hat costing $30.00 is to be given a mark-up of 45% on retail.
    The retail should be
    A. $43.50   B. $46.40   C. $55.40   D. $54.50

    17.____

18. Retail price $40 per unit; mark-up 40% of retail; transportation charge, $1 per unit.
    Find billed cost that store can pay.
    A. 23   B. $24   C. $23.75   D. $24.75

    18.____

19. A buyer plans to spend $17,000 at retail for merchandise at a mark-up of 34%. He finds a special value at $3,000 that he can sell for $6,000.
What mark-up percentage does he need on the balance of his purchases in order to achieve his planned 34%?
    A. 35 B. 19.9 C. 15 D. 22.5

20. A store has a gross margin of 40% and reductions of 13%. Cash discount on purchases are not credited to the department. There are no alteration costs.
What is the initial mark-up?
    A. 46% B. 53% C. 27% D. 26%

21. A dress is to retail for $35 with a mark-up of 40% of retail.
The cost of the dress to the retailer was
    A. $25 B. $21 C. $14 D. $20

22. The cost is $1.20 and the desired gross profit is 40% of retail.
The retail price should be
    A. $1.60 B. $1.68 C. $2.00 D. $2.40

23. The realized mark-up on a TV set is $50. The mark-up is 25% of retail.
The cost of the TV set to the retailer was
    A. $200 B. $125 C. $100 D. $150

24. Farnum, a salesman, earns $19.20 per hour for 40 hours a week, with time and a half for all hours over 40 per week. Last week, his total earnings were $940.80.
How many hours did he work last week?
    A. 46 B. 49 C. 47 D. 48

25. Dane & Clarke, partners, share profits in a 5:3 ratio. Dane's share of the profit for this year was $12,000 more than Clarke's share.
Clarke's share of the net profit was
    A. $30,000 B. $48,000 C. $36,000 D. $18,000

KEY (CORRECT ANSWERS)

1.	C	11.	A
2.	D	12.	B
3.	A	13.	C
4.	C	14.	D
5.	A	15.	C
6.	C	16.	A
7.	B	17.	D
8.	D	18.	A
9.	A	19.	B
10.	A	20.	A

21. B
22. C
23. D
24. A
25. D

SOLUTIONS TO PROBLEMS

1. 5 + 5 – 1 = 9%. Then, (40%)(91) = 36.4%.

2. (25)($150) = $3,750, and $3,750 ÷ .625 = $6000 total selling price of all sets. $6,000 – (20)($265) = $700; 700 ÷ 5 = $140 selling price for each of the last 5 sets. Markdown amount = $265 - $140 = $125.

3. When the article's original selling price was $12, its cost was $8.00. If the article's original selling price were to be $10, it would cost $(8.00)/12.00×10.00) = $6.67.

4. Resulting percentage = (1.20)(1-.10) = .72 = 72%.

5. ($45)(.40) = $18 + .65 = $18.65. Then, ($18.65)(.9091) = $16.95, closest to $16.96 in American currency.

6. 40 – 4½ - 5¾ - 6⅞ = 22⅞ yds.

7. 76½ ÷ 2½ = 30.6, rounded down to 30 shirts.

8. 24.5 – 1.003 = 23.497.

9. ($265,830)(.0525) = $13,956.09.

10. $67,507.50 ÷ $22.50 = 3,000 transactions.

11. $275,825,000 ÷ .945 = $291,878,000.

12. $50,000,000 + $1,500,000 - $10,000,000 = $37,500,000 = $4,000,000.
    Then, $4,000,000 ÷ $50,000,000 = .08 = 8%.

13. An increase of 300% over x = 4x, so sales are 4 times as large.

14. Gross sales = $374,000 ÷ .85 = $440,000.

15. (1.05)(1.03) = 1.0815, which represents an 8.15% increase in dollar sales volume.

16. $525 - $310 = $215; then, $215/$525 = 40.9%.

17. $30 will represent 55% of retail amount. Thus, retail will be $30 ÷ .55 = $54.50.

18. ($40)(.60) - $1 = $23.

19. ($17,000)(1.34) = $22,780. Then, $22,780 - $6000 = $16,780. Also, $17,000 - $3,000 = $14,000. Finally, ($16,780 - $14,000) ÷ $14,000 ≈ 19.9%.

20. Let x = markup percent. Then, x – 40/x = .13. Solving, x = 46.

21. Cost = ($35)(.60) = $21.

22. Let x = retail price. Then, $1.20 = .60x. Solving, x = $2.00.

23. $50 = 25% of retail, so retail = $200. Thus, cost = $200 - $50 = $150.

24. Let x = overtime hours. Then, ($19.20)(40) + $28.80x = $940.80. Solving, x = 6 total.

25. 5x = 3x - $12,000. So, x = $6,000. Clarke's share = (3)($6,000) = $18,000.

TEST 2

DIRECTIONS: Each question or incomplete statement is followed by several suggested answers or completions. Select the one that BEST answers the question or completes the statement. *PRINT THE LETTER OF THE CORRECT ANSWER IN THE SPACE AT THE RIGHT.*

1. Assume that you require 77 dozen felt practice golf balls.
   Which of the following represents the LOWEST bid for these balls?
   A. 41¢ per half-dozen less a 3% discount
   B. 83¢ per dozen less a 7½% discount
   C. 85¢ per dozen less a 10% discount
   D. $65.00 less a series discount of 3%, 2%

   1.____

2. Assume that you require 1,944 rulers, packed 12 to the box, 18 boxes to the carton.
   Which of the following represents the LOWEST bid for these rulers?
   A. 5½ ¢ per ruler
   B. 6¢ for the first 750 rulers; 5½¢ for the next 750 rulers; 4½¢ for every ruler thereafter
   C. $11.85 per carton
   D. $110 less series discounts of 2%, 1%.

   2.____

3. Assume that you require 20 cartons of colored raffia, cellophane wrapped in one lb. packages, 50 packages to the carton.
   Which of the following represents the LOWEST bid for the raffia?
   A. 8¢ per lb.; 15¢ per carton packaging charge; 20¢ per carton delivery charge
   B. 9¢ per lb. less a 3% discount
   C. 10¢ per lb. for the first 150 lbs.; 9¢ per lb. for the next 200 lbs.; 80 for each lb. thereafter
   D. $83.50 less a 4½% discount

   3.____

4. Assume that you require 50 yards of table felt, 48" wide, and 12 yards of table felt, 72" wide.
   Which of the following represents the LOWEST bid for this felt?
   A. 32¢ per yard (48" wide), 40¢ per yard (72" wide)
   B. 34¢ per yard (48" wide), 43¢ per yard (72" wide); series discounts of 5%, 3%
   C. 360 per yard (48" wide), 41¢ per yard (72" wide); 8% discount, packing charge 75¢
   D. $23.00 for the order, 9% discount, packing charge 50¢

   4.____

5. If the cost of 3 erasers is 5¢, the cost of 2½ dozen erasers is
   A. 18¢   B. 37½¢   C. 50¢   D. 31½¢

   5.____

109

6. A circle graph of a budget shows the expenditure of 26.2% for housing, 28.4% for food, 12% for clothing, 12.7% for taxes, and the balance for miscellaneous items.
   The percent for miscellaneous items is
   A. 31.5   B. 79.3   C. 20.7   D. 68.5

7. The cost of a broadloom rug measuring 4 feet by 6 feet, at $6.30 per square yard, is
   A. $16.80   B. $50.40   C. $37.60   D. $21.00

8. The number of tiles each measuring 2 inches by 3 inches needed for a wall 3 feet high and 5 feet long is
   A. 180   B. 30   C. 360   D 60

9. Assume that you require 4 tons of fertilizer. The fertilizer is packed in 100 pound bags.
   Which of the following represents the LOWEST bid for the fertilizer?
   A. 6¢ per pound
   B. $5.50 per bag
   C. $7.00 for each of the first 30 bags; $5.00 for each bag thereafter
   D. $500.00 less 3½% discount

10. Assume pencils are packed 5 gross to the case. A buyer requires 3,800 pencils each for three departments and 2,700 pencils for another department. Assume that the vendor will ship unbroken cases only directly to each department.
    How many cases should he buy?
    A. 21   B. 22   C. 48   D. 49

11. Assume that a buyer had to purchase 40,000 lbs. of salt.
    Which one of the following bids should he accept, assuming quality, service, and delivery terms are all the same?
    A. 1¢ per pound, 2%-30 days
    B. 99¢ per 100 lbs., 1%-30 days
    C. $19 per ton, 1%-30 days
    D. $18 per ton, net-30 days

12. Which one of the following four bids represent the BEST value, assuming delivery costs amount to $100?
    A. $1,000 f.o.b. buyer, less 2%-10 days
    B. $900 f.o.b. seller, less 2%-10 days
    C. $975 delivered, net cash 30 days
    D. $990 f.o.b. buyer, less 1%-10 days

13. Suppose that four suppliers make the following offers to sell 2,000 units of a particular commodity.
    Which one is the MOST advantageous proposal?
    A. $10 list, less 40% and 5%
    B. $5 cost, plus 20% to cover overhead and profit
    C. $10 list, less 20% and 20%
    D. $5 cost, plus 10% overhead and 10% for profit

3 (#2)

14. Suppose that you purchase 100 units of an item at a list of $1 per unit less 40% and 10%, and less 2% if paid within 10 days.
    If payment is made within the 10-day limit, the amount of the payment should be
    A. $52.92   B. $54.00   C. $58.80   D. $60.00

    14.____

15. Assume that the 2018 cost of living factor was 100 and that a certain product was selling that year for $5 per unit. Assume further that at the present time the cost of living factor is 150.
    If the selling price of the product increased 10% more than the cost of living during this period, at the present time the product would be selling for _____ per unit.
    A. $8.25   B. $10.50   C. $16.50   D. $7.75

    15.____

16. A certain food is sold in 4 ounce cans at 10 for $1.00 and in 1 pound cans at 3 for $1.00.
    The savings in price per ounce by purchasing the food in the larger can is _____ cents/ounce.
    A. .53   B. .35   C. .42   D. .68

    16.____

17. After an article is discounted at 25%, it sells for $375.
    The ORIGINAL price of the article was
    A. $93.75   B. $350   C. $35   D $500

    17.____

18. Assume that you require 1,440 pencils, packed 12 to the box, 24 boxes to the carton.
    Which of the following represents the LOWEST bid for these pencils?
    A. 2¢ per pencil
    B. $6.50 per carton
    C. 27¢ per box less a 4% discount
    D. $40 less a 3% discount

    18.____

19. If erasers cost 8¢ each for the first 250, 70 each for the next 250, and 5¢ for every eraser thereafter, how many erasers may be purchased for $50?
    A. 600   B. 750   C. 850   D. 1,000

    19.____

20. Assume that a buyer saves $14 on the purchase of an item that is discounted at 25%
    The amount of money that the buyer must pay for the item is
    A. $42   B. $52   C. $54   D. $56

    20.____

Questions 21-24.

DIRECTIONS: Questions 21 through 24 are to be answered on the basis of the following method of obtaining a reorder point: multiply the monthly rate of consumption by the lead time (in months) and add the minimum balance.

21. If the lead time is one-half month, the minimum balance is 6 units, and the monthly rate of consumption is 4 units, then the reorder point is _____ units.
    A. 4   B. 6   C. 8   D. 12

    21.____

22. If the reorder point is 25 units, the lead time is 3 months, and the minimum balance is 10 units, then the average monthly rate of consumption is _____ units.
   A. 3   B. 5   C. 6   D. 10

23. If the reorder point is 400 units, the lead time is 2 months, and the monthly rate of consumption is 150 units, then the minimum balance is _____ units.
   A. 50   B. 100   C. 150   D. 200

24. If the reorder point is 75 units, the monthly rate of consumption is 60 units, and the minimum balance is 45 units, then the lead time is _____ month(s).
   A. ½   B. 1   C. 2   D. 4

25. A purchasing office has 4,992 special requisitions to be processed. Working alone, Buyer A could process these in 30 days; working alone, Buyer B could process these in 40 days; working alone, Buyer C could process these in 60 days.
   The LEAST number of days in which Buyers A, B, and C working together can process these 4,992 special requisitions is APPROXIMATELY _____ days.
   A. 14   B. 20   C. 34   D. 45

KEY (CORRECT ANSWERS)

1.	C		11.	D
2.	B		12.	C
3.	D		13.	A
4.	B		14.	A
5.	C		15.	A
6.	C		16.	C
7.	A		17.	D
8.	C		18.	A
9.	B		19.	B
10.	B		20.	A

21. C
22. B
23. B
24. A
25. A

SOLUTIONS TO PROBLEMS

1. Bid A = (.82)(77)(.97) ≈ $61.25
   Bid B = (.83)(77)(.925) ≈ $59.12
   Bid C = (.85)(77)(.90) ≈ $58.91
   Bid D = ($65.00)(.97)(.98) ≈ $61.79.
   Thus, Bid C is lowest.

2. Bid A = (.055)(1944) = $106.92
   Bid B = (.06)(750) + (.055)(750) + (.045)(444) = $106.23
   Bid C = ($11.85)(9) = $106.65
   Bid D = ($110)(.98)(.99) ≈ $106.72.
   Thus, Bid B is lowest.

3. Bid A = (.08)(1000) + (.15)(20) + (.20)(20) = $87.00
   Bid B = (.09)(1000) = $87.30
   Bid C = (.10)(150) + (.09)(200) + (.08)(650) = $85.00
   Bid D = ($83.50)(.955) ≈ $79.74
   Thus, Bid D is lowest.

4. Bid A = (.32)(50) + (.40)(12) = $20.80
   Bid B = (.34)(50) + (.43)(12) = $22.16; so ($22.16)(.95)(.97) ≈ $20.42
   Bid C = (.36)(50) + (.41)(12) = $22.92; so ($22.92)(.92) + .75 ≈ $21.84
   Bid D = ($23.00)(.91) + .50 = $21.43
   Bid B is lowest.

5. (2½)(12) = 30 erasers, which will cost (.05)(10) = 50¢

6. 100 − 26.2 − 28.4 − 12 − 12.7 = 20.7% for miscellaneous items.

7. 24 ÷ 9 = $2^{2}/_{3}$ sq. yds. Then, ($6.30)($2^{2}/_{3}$) = $16.80

8. 3'2" = 18; 5'3" = 20. Thus, (18)(20) = 360 tiles.

9. Bid A = (.06)(8000) = $480
   Bid B = ($5.50)(80) = $440
   Bid C = ($7.00)(30) + ($5.00)(50) = $460
   Bid D = ($500)(.965) = $482.59
   Thus, Bid B is lowest.

10. 5 gross = 5(144); 3800 will be 6 unbroken cases × 3 = 18.
                    2700 will be 4 unbroken cases   = 4
                                                                      22

11. Bid A = (.01)(40,000)(.98) = $392.00
    Bid B = (.99)(400)(.99) = $392.04
    Bid C = ($19)(20)(.99) = $376.20
    Bid D = ($18)(20) = $360.00
    Bid D is lowest.

12. A. 1,000 – 2% = 980
    B. 900 + 100 – 2% = 980
    C. 975
    D. 990 – 9.90 = 980.10
    C is best value.

13. Proposal A: ($10)(.60)(.95) = $5.70
    Proposal B: $5 + ($5)(.20) = $6.00
    Proposal C: ($10)(.80)(.80) = $6.40
    Proposal D: $5 + (.20)($5) = $6.00
    Proposal A is lowest.

14. Payment = ($100)(.60)(.90)(.98) = $52.92

15. Present cost = ($5)(1.50)(1.10) = $8.25

16. 40 ounces for $1.00 in smaller cans means 2.5 cents per ounce. For the larger cans, (3)(16) = 48 ounces for $1.00, which means 2.083 cents per ounce. The savings is approximately .42 cents per ounce.

17. Original price − $375 ÷ 75 = $500

18. Bid A = (1440)(.02) = $28.80
    Bid B = (1440 ÷ 288)($6.50) = $32.50
    Bid C = [(144 ÷ 12)(.27)][.96] = $31.10
    Bid D = ($40)(.97) = $38.80
    Bid A is lowest.

19. 250 erasers cost (250)(.08) = $20
    500 erasers cost $20 + (250)(.07) = $37.50
    The number of additional erasers = ($50 - $37.50) ÷ .05 = 250
    Total number of erasers = 750

20. $14 ÷ .25 = $56. Then, $56 - $14 = $42

21. (4)(.5) + 6 = 8 units

22. Let x = monthly rate. Then, (x)(3) + 10 = 25. Solving, x = 5 units.

23. Let x = minimum balance. (150)(2) + x = 400. Solving, x = 100 units.

24. Let x = lead time. (60)(x) + 45 = 75. Solving, x = ½ month.

25. Buyer A does 4992 ÷ 30 ≈ 166 per day.
Buyer B does 4992 ÷ 40 ≈ 125 per day.
Buyer C does 4992 ÷ 60 ≈ 83 per day.
Working together, approximately 374 requisitions are done per day.
Finally, 4992 ÷ 374 ≈ 13, closest to 14 in selections.